Mt. Desert Island and Acadia National Park

AN INFORMAL HISTORY

MT. DESERT ISLAND

MAINE

Mt. Desert Island and Acadia National Park

AN INFORMAL HISTORY

Photographs and Text
by Sargent F. Collier

Revised and Edited by G.W. Helfrich

DOWN EAST MAGAZINE
Camden, Maine

Copyright © 1978 by Eleanor McC. Collier

Designed by Ingrid Beckman

Library of Congress Catalogue Card Number
78-66726

First Edition
ISBN 0-89272-044-1

Printed in the United States of America

Acknowledgments

This volume is a distillation of three books of words and photographs by the late Sargent Collier — in the order of their publication, *Mount Desert: The Most Beautiful Island in the World* (1952), *Green Grows Bar Harbor* (1964), and *Acadia National Park: George B. Dorr's Triumph* (1965).

All three have been out of print for some time and in recent years have become collector's items, at least locally. They have been combined in the present volume to meet the demand of those who wanted to read them again and, it is hoped, will appeal to a new generation of readers who have fallen under the spell of Mt. Desert Island.

With the passage of years time has worked changes, and it has been necessary to edit, revise, and in some cases add to, the text. Here, I am especially grateful to Gladys O'Neil of the Bar Harbor Historical Society who helped me to check and bring up to date much of the material. I should like to thank also Robert Rothe, naturalist of the Acadia National Park staff, William L. Dupuy of the Jackson Laboratory, Dr. William B. Kinter of the Mt. Desert Island Biological Laboratory, and Paul Beltramini, College of the Atlantic.

For permission to quote from Richard Hale's *The Story of Bar Harbor,* our thanks to Ives Washburn, Inc., New York; for permission to quote from Samuel Eliot Morison's *The Story of Mt. Desert Island,* to Little, Brown & Company, Boston; and for permission to quote from Cleveland Amory's *The Last Resorts,* to Harper & Row, New York.

G. W. Helfrich

Bar Harbor, Maine
1978

Table of Contents

Acadiana

"Spruce is a goodly tree of which they make Masts for Ships and Sail Yards. It is generally conceived by those who have skill in Building of Ships that here is absolutely the best trees in the World, many of them being three Fathom about and of great length."

Josselyn. New England's Rarities Discovered, 1672

One Fir only grows in the Acadian Forest:

The Balsam Fir, Abies balsamea, which can readily be distinguished from the resembling Spruces by its smooth, blistered bark and the way in which its needles are borne in flat, horizontal rows on the branchlets, and are silvery beneath, while those of the Spruces are disposed irregularly around the branchlets and are alike in color on all sides.

Another distinction, easily observed in its season, between the Firs and Spruces in all species is that the Fir Trees carry their cones upright, like Christmas candles, closely bunched together near the tree top, while the Spruces carry theirs turned downward and scattered over top and branches. The Balsam Fir is a beautiful tree when young and grows rapidly, but ages soon. Its dead needles heated by the sun, become pungently aromatic.

Silva of North America

Wild flowers are abundant from early spring, when the Trailing Arbutus or Mayflower puts forth its blossoms, till the Witch Hazel blooms in fall, scattering as it flowers its long-held seed. Orchids of the terrestrial species grow freely in beautiful and interesting forms, culminating in display at mid-summer in the superb Fringed Orchid with its pale purple flowers. The pure white Trillium with deep purple blotches, the Clintonia, forming great beds of splendid foliage in the woods, the Wild Iris and the Cardinal Flower along the banks of streams, the native Lilies, growing among beds of ferns, the decorative Twisted Stalk with brick-red, pendent fruit, the Hairbell, clinging to cliffs and ledges by the sea, the delicate Linnea, the brilliant-fruiting Dwarf Cornel, the springtime Violets, the summer Roses and the autumn Asters, the Blueberries and Wild Strawberries, the Raspberries and Blackberries, the Shad Bush and the Thorn, the Viburnum, most beautiful of northern woodland shrubs, the Rhodora, sung by Emerson, the Sumach and the Mountain Ash — there is no period the season through that lacks its special interest of flower or fruit.

Silva of North America. Published in 1897

The exposed headlands and bogs of the Mount Desert region support between two and three hundred species of plants which are typical of the arctic, subarctic, and Hudsonian regions of America, and which on the eastern coast of New England or the alpine summits of the White Mountains reach their actual or approximate southern limits — such plants, for instance, as the Black Crowberry, Empetrum nigrum; the Baked-apple Berry, Rubus Chamaemorus; the Creeping Juniper, Juniperus horizontalis; the Greenland Sandwort, Arenaria groenlandica; the Rose-root, Sedum roseum; and the Banksian Pine, Pinus Banksiana.

But the flora of the Mount Desert region is not by any means entirely arctic or subarctic. There we find essentially all the common plants of the Canadian zone, and mingling with them in sheltered nooks and meadows or on warm slopes, many scores of plants which reach their extreme northern or northeastern limit on Mount Desert or the immediate coast — such plants as the Pitch Pine, Pinus rigida; the Bear Oak, Quercus ilicifolia; the Sweet Pepperbush, Clethra alnifolia; the Swamp Loosestrife, Decodon verticillatus; the Meadow Beauty, Rhexia virginica; and the Maple-leaved Viburnum, acerifolium.

In its rock and soil composition Mount Desert offers a most attractive possibility. Much of the Island consists of granite rocks, with the consequent acid soils that these give rise to; but the soils derived from some of the metamorphic series, slates and shales, are, judging from the native vegetation, of a basic or even limy character, and many of the swamps are covered not with the heath thickets of acid bogs but with the characteristic grasses and sedges of sweet areas.

A number of the Island plants, indeed, sometimes of rock habitats, sometimes of swamps, suggest themselves at once as species which, in their wide range, show a strong preference for sweet or limy habitats: the Shrubby Cinquefoil, Potentilla fruticoas; the Showy Lady's Slipper, Cypripedium hirsutum; the Hemlock Parsley, Coniosèlinum chinense, are instances.

"An Acadia Plant Sanctuary"
Prof. M. L. Fernald

The wild pear as we call it here, Amelanchier canadensis, a wild plum really, has made a scene of surpassing loveliness on the Park motor road to Jordan Pond during this past week. It has long-petalled, pure white blossoms, clustered in masses, with foliage of a soft springtime red just breaking through, giving a contrasting color-background to the blossoms.

From Dorr letter to Director,
U.S. National Park Service, Washington, D.C.

Preface

Sargent Collier's family has lived in Maine and Massachusetts ever since the former was part of the latter. After graduation from Harvard in 1926, he worked in advertising, public relations and as a writer; he was joint owner and editor of *The Writer* and his work appeared in many other publications.

During World War II, he was trained as a photographer by the United States Navy, and from that point on his work was, as he stated it, "with lens and pen." In addition to the three books represented in this volume, Sarge was the author of *Down East*, an account in pictures and text of an odyssey that took him from Camden, Maine to the city of Quebec — by way of Prince Edward Island, Nova Scotia and the Gaspe. He achieved a widespread reputation as a photographer, not only of the northeast, but of Mexico, Kentucky and Florida as well.

He often said that there wasn't enough time for all the things he wanted to do. There wasn't. How fortunate that he left the legacy of his four books, his travel writing, his photographs. The books that have been revised and edited into this one volume — *Mt. Desert — Most Beautiful Island in the World, Green Grows Bar Harbor,* and *Acadia National Park — The Triumph of George Dorr,* have not lost their original combination of humor and lightness, awareness of and ability to capture the beauty of the island. These qualities were Sargent Collier's hallmark and his legacy to us.

E. M. C.

Balance Rock, off the Bar Harbor shore path, one of the numerous pebbles deposited by the glacier centuries ago. Nudged by the sea, the big stone over the decades has moved its position, without losing its balance.

Islands, Indians and Explorers

MOUNT Desert is the third largest island on the coast of continental United States. Its 107.77 square miles are overshadowed by the 1254 of Long Island, N.Y., the largest, but very close to Martha's Vineyard, Mass., in second place with 108.

Mount Desert is five times larger than Manhattan and has six times the area of winter resort Bermuda. It is almost twice the size of Staten Island and Catalina.

Of all the coastal islands, only one other, Orcas in Puget Sound, can claim a mountain range, a number of lakes and a giant fjord, such as Somes Sound.

Mount Desert is well Down East — only 133 miles from Eastport on the country's watery, easternmost frontier.

Some claim Mt. Katahdin's 5,268 ft. peak, 100 miles due north and a favorite view from Mt. Cadillac, is the first spot in the United States touched by the morning sun in summer. But two groups of University of Maine students, stationed on both summits, awarded the distinction to Mt. Cadillac itself. Possibly the seasonal declination of the sun causes some variance.

From earliest record, Mount Desert has been a landfall for transatlantic mariners. Cadillac Mountain, highest promontory on the Atlantic coast north of Rio de Janeiro, must have been sighted by the Norsemen around 1000 A. D. Giovanni da Verazzano, an Italian sailing in the service of France who discovered Manhattan and Nantucket, noted it in 1500. It was Verazzano who coined the name Acadia, based on an Abenaki Indian word. More than four centuries later, in 1929, the name was given to Acadia National Park on Mount Desert — first national park east of the Mississippi and the first in the United States to cost the taxpayers nothing. All the land was donated to the government by generous and farsighted citizens.

Samuel de Champlain discovered the island in 1604 and named it for a few bald peaks, *l'Isle des Monts-deserts*. But with its heavily forested slopes, lakes, ponds and streams, nothing could less resemble a desert. More than five hundred kinds of flowering plants grow on the island and many types of ferns, mosses, lichens, and lesser plants. In this Eden there are no poisonous snakes.

Not far in Champlain's wake came Henry Hudson, to cut a tall tree for a mast and to reward the friendliness of the aborigines with cruelty; Captain John Smith, soldier-sailor extraordinary, in 1617 marked the island's hills and mountains on the margin of his celebrated map of New England; John Winthrop wrote in his journal of 1630 of the ecstasy of Arabella's weary company when they sighted the Mount Desert hills and smelt the fragrance of the spruces.

A motor bridge across Mount Desert Narrows at Trenton spans a slender thread of water to the north; this tidal area spared Mount Desert from the drab estate of a peninsula and preserved its romantic status as an island. Yet one would not need the strength of George Washington to skim a coin across at low tide. However, the rest of its 75-mile periphery is bordered by the deep sea. It is bounded on the east by Frenchman Bay, on the south by Pemesquit Bay and the Atlantic Ocean and on the west by Blue Hill Bay.

Mount Desert, incidentally, is one of the few places in New England which makes no claim of Washington having slept there. But many of the famous have. Lafayette is reported to have courted during a visit to the island, and according to a persistent piece of gossip, Talleyrand was born at Southwest Harbor. The story insists that Tallyrand's birth certificate was forged to cover unconventional circumstances of his Mount Desert nativity. At least he is known to have voyaged to the area. Talleyrand Cottage was the name given in the 1890's to an imposing gabled block of the Malvern Hotel all of which was destroyed in the Bar Harbor fire.

A completely undocumented but nonetheless a provocative story that has come down the years is, that somewhere along our coast, or in Canada, Lord Nelson, as a midshipman, overstayed a shore leave for amorous reasons and that it almost caused his expulsion from the Royal Navy. How seriously this might have changed the world's history must remain a matter of speculation. History, although generally free with Nelson's European meanderings, could in this case be understandably vague. Mount Desert may have been where the great sea lord strayed.

Jutting as it does so far out to sea, naturally the earliest approaches to Mount Desert were by water. Automobiles were not permitted on the island until 1915. It is still an area of white sails. Northeast Harbor, facetiously called Philadelphia-by-The-Sea, because such a large percentage of its summer residents hail from the City of Brotherly Love, has a racing fleet second only to Marblehead, Mass.

Next to summer folk, the island's most successful industries are science laboratories, it is the site of the Jackson Laboratory and the Mt. Desert Biological Laboratory, boat building and fishing with the accent on lobstering.

Ornithologists appreciate the island's mixture of predominantly Canadian birds and an increasing southern element. And to the delight of botanists, the region supports over 200 species of arctic, subarctic, and Hudsonian flora; essentially all the common plants of the Canadian zone; and scores of plants which reach their northernmost limits on Mt. Desert.

Geologists admire the area for its toughness. At one time the mountains may have stood as high as the Alps and extended perhaps 80 miles farther out to sea. Although crushed by the forces of the millennia the peaks stood too tall to be depressed to the level of the mainland. Likewise when the glacial sheet was laid upon it, such as covers Greenland today, the island withstood the onslaught just as it did the flames of 1947; however, many valleys were turned into long arms of the

Near Somesville from Babson's Bridge where Kittredge brook feeds into Somes Sound . . . Paradise Point at right opposite Somesville's own balance rock . . . Acadia Mountain in the distance.

sea — lakes were artistically deposited between mountains; hills severed from the mainland became small islands.

Collectors of precious stones find in the pink granite shores brilliantly colored microlite and amazonite, also used locally in jewelry. There are only two other deposits of amazonite in the United States — Amelia Court House, Virginia, and Pikes Peak, Colorado.

For the earliest and longest association with the island, homage must be paid to the fleur-de-lis. Because of the Cadillac and de Gregoire grants, Mount Desert is the only place in the United States, except Louisiana, where real estate titles must be traced back to the French crown.

Whereas, French mariner-cartographer Champlain named the island, he was also the first to confuse us with its pronunciation. Most residents pronounce the name as it is read from a menu; some, possibly more correctly, as in the Desert of Sahara. Pronounce it what you will — DEZZ-ert, Desair, or Des-URT — Henry van Dyke and other writers have called it, "The Most Beautiful Island in the World."

The Indians who arrived long before the French called it Pemetic (sloping land). They thought it resembled the claw of a crab or a lobster, possibly because of the sharp-toothed jaws holding Somes Sound — an appropriate symbol since today the salty islanders participate most actively in lobstering. (Maine's coastal waters produce an annual 20 million lbs. of lobsters, 75% of the nation's total.)

The French explorers considered the Indians along this section of the coast of a superior strain and they won the friendship and loyalty of the aborigines by accepting them as virtual equals.

They joined the red men in the hunt and on the warpath and each learned much of the other's skills. The French became adept at the Indian's hit-and-run technique, while the English paid dearly for stubborn adherence to the formality of European battlefield tactics.

Many Frenchmen, even those at home in Paris salons, took Indian brides, an outstanding example being the Baron de St. Castin, for whom Castine is named. He married an Indian princess, daughter of Chief Madockawando, and the status of their four children was unquestioned by French society.

There is a distinct parallel between the Indians who frequented Mount Desert and the later summer visitors. The Indians considered summers spent here the most agreeable part of their lives. They, with considerable justification, regarded the island as a health resort and brought along their old people from the mainland to build up their strength against the winter.

In spring they loaded the family canoe and paddled out to set up bark wigwams on the same lot as the previous year. Then they settled down to dig clams and fish and to enjoy a good measure of leisure.

At a date roughly conforming to our day-after-Labor-Day, they returned to their palisaded winter villages at Kadesquit, on the Penobscot near present-day Bangor. After harvesting pumpkins, corn and beans planted before the island sojourn, and settling their families, the hunting season called the braves back to the island, where they lived on an abundance of ducks, geese and other waterfowl.

The routine was not greatly different from that of many present citizenry. Historian Henry Parkman thus describes the island's first summer colonists:

"Their summer stay at the seashore was perhaps the most pleasant, and certainly the most picturesque, part of their lives. Bivouacked by some of the innumerable coves and inlets that indent these coasts, they passed their days in that alternation of indolence and action which is second nature to the Indian. Here in wet weather, while the torpid water was dimpled with raindrops, and the upturned canoes lay idle on the pebbles, the listless warrior smoked his pipe under his roof of bark, or launched his slender craft at the dawn of the July day, when shores and islands were painted in shadow against the rosy east, and forests, dusky and cool, lay waiting for the sunrise. The women gathered raspberries, or whortleberries in the open places of the woods, or clams and oysters in the sands and shallows, adding their shells as contribution to the shellheaps that have accumulated for ages along these shores. The men fished, speared porpoises, or shot seals."

The largest shellheaps are at Manchester's Point, showing this was the Indians' favorite summer rendezvous. Other villages were located at Hull's Cove and Goose Cove. The athletic field at Bar Harbor, formerly called Squaw Hollow, was the location of an Indian settlement.

Here sleeps Mme. Barthelemy de Gregoire and her husband, who once claimed all Mount Desert. The stone is in the village cemetery at Hull's Cove. (Right) The Champlain monument near Seal Harbor.

When the first white summer visitors came to Mount Desert, Indians still were trapping mink and muskrat on the island and there was a spruce bough encampment at Somes Pond where their women told fortunes. Clad in plaid shawls and shiny beaver hats, the squaws also peddled baskets and fine beadwork.

Now most of the Indians in this part of Maine dwell in reservations at Old Town, a sixty-mile drive from Mount Desert, and at Pleasant Point, near Eastport and the Canadian border.

On Mount Desert Island Indian relics are assembled at the little Abbe Museum, which stands by the Sieur de Monts Spring in Acadia National Park, between Bar Harbor and Otter Creek. ("Crick," if employing the autochthonous pronunciation.)

Champlain

SAMUEL de Champlain was the beau ideal among navigators when the western hemisphere was largely an unopened oyster.

Champlain possessed such a charming personality that historians almost invariably dwell upon it in recording that he was an explorer and geographer of extraordinary talent. Relying upon a nice understanding of the celestial sphere, he went boldly upon unknown waters; as master of the crude nautical instruments of the day, he made such accurate charts that they could be relied upon by today's mariner.

His zeal is best described in the dedication of one of his books:

"Among the most useful and excellent arts, navigation has always seemed to me to take the first place. In the measure that it is dangerous and accompanied by a thousand perils, by so much is it honorable and lifted above all other arts, being in no wise suitable for those who lack courage and confidence. By this art we acquire knowledge of various lands, countries and kingdoms. By it we bring home all sorts of riches, by it the idolatry of Paganism is overthrown and Christianity declared in all parts of the earth. It is this art that has from my childhood lured me to love it, and has caused me to expose myself almost all my life to the rude waves of the ocean."

Champlain came to Mount Desert in 1604, or sixteen years before the Pilgrims landed at Plymouth, but he did not tarry. He was on a voyage of exploration and discovery and he pursued that quest with more enthusiasm than a

Rivaling the northern lights, the moon climbs out of the eastern sea, over Frenchman Bay. The clouds cooperated in producing this moonshade from Ocean Drive.

yachtsman on a summer cruise. He could leave the prosaic business of founding settlements to others.

Says John Fiske in his *New France and New England:*

"He was a true Viking who loved the tossing waves and the howling of the winds in the shrouds. He was a strict disciplinarian but courteous and merciful. In the whole course of French history there are few personages so attractive."

So it is not surprising that when the Sieur de Monts, bearing the title Lieutenant General of New France, sailed to possess and settle that part of North America between the fortieth and forty-sixth parallels of latitude he enlisted Champlain as his pilot and cartographer.

De Monts' company was as ill-assorted an aggregation as ever put to sea. It included nobles from the court of Henry IV, miscreants from Paris prisons, Catholic priests and Huguenot ministers, ruffians and young volunteers of high birth and character. Hope of personal gain probably inspired the majority, spurred on by rumors an Eldorado was hidden in a land where Indians existed in mean poverty. There is little to indicate Champlain shared his shipmates' motives.

De Monts founded a settlement at the mouth of the St. Croix River, but Champlain pushed on, with fourteen men, including two friendly Indians as interpreters. Their craft was a small, open vessel of about seventeen tons, equipped with lateen sails and oars. This is his own account of that voyage:

"Setting out from the mouth of the St. Croix and sailing westward along the coast, the same day [September 5, 1604] we passed near to an island some four or five leagues long, in the neighborhood of which we just escaped being lost on a rock that was just awash and which made a hole in the bottom of our boat. From this island to the mainland on the north the distance is not more than a hundred paces [site of Trenton Bridge]. The island is high and notched in places so that from the sea it gives the appearance of a range of seven or eight mountains. The summits are all bare and rocky. The slopes are covered with pines, firs and birches. I named it *l'isle des Monts-deserts.*"

Champlain described the island so clearly that future voyagers readily recognized it. His actual landing place is in dispute. It could have been Otter Creek, near Seal Harbor, but it probably was at Cromwell Harbor, just below the Porcupine Islands which guard Bar Harbor. There the Jesuit expedition stopped briefly nine years later, and Cadillac anchored in 1688.*

When Champlain wrote that he had loved the sea from childhood, he did not exaggerate. Son of a captain in the Royal Navy of France and born in 1567 on Biscay Bay, he was familiar with sailing vessels from boyhood. He visited the West Indies, Panama and Mexico long before he saw North America. With sword in one hand and the cross in the other, he became father of Canada. This ardent champion of the fleur-de-lis died on the rock of Quebec on Christmas Day, 1635, content to draw his last breath in the wilderness, where he had "always desired to see the Lily flourish and also the true religion, Catholic, Apostolic and Roman."

*The American authority, not only of this Island's history but of its origins across the seas and of its maritime explorers and wars, Admiral Samuel Eliot Morison, who summered on Mt. Desert, asserts that Champlain arrived here in a patache, a square rigged ketch of seventeen tons. In his delightful little book, "The Story of Mount Desert Island" (Little, Brown, 1960) Morison suggests that Champlain hit the ledge off Otter cliffs (now marked by a bell buoy) and thence proceeded into Otter Creek for repairs. Morison doubts that Champlain sailed further up Frenchman Bay to the Narrows, more likely being content with the word of the Indians that he lay in waters surrounding a mammoth island.

Hail and Farewell to the Jesuits

IT probably was not then apparent, but when the heavy hand of Captain Samuel Argall fell on the Jesuit mission on Mount Desert, the curtain was rung down on French ambitions in North America.

Ironically, fall of the settlement was speeded by Indians, who failed to recognize the English as enemies of their French friends, and so betrayed them, thus perhaps changing the course of history.

Madame de Guercheville, a lady of wise and winsome charm, close enough to the court to command attention, had backed the project with her own wealth. Three years she planned and prepared for the expedition and, aided by ladies of the court, embroidered intricate altar cloths for use in the New World. She had been impressed by the success of a Jesuit Mission in Paraguay and was eager to found a religious paradise in North America.

From the impoverished Sieur de Monts, Madame de Guercheville obtained patents to lands in Acadia, and she also acquired the little ship *Jonas,* which had formerly flown de Monts' flag.

Aboard, when the *Jonas* cleared Honfleur March 12, 1613, were sixteen priests and a number of lay brothers, forty-eight prospective settlers, artisans and laborers, and some horses and goats. A brief call was made at Port Royal to take aboard additional priests.

The voyagers' intended destination was a location on Penobscot called Kadesquit, recommended highly by Champlain. But off Mount Desert they encountered fog so terrifying it evoked prayers for deliverance. (A sundrenched Bar Harborite would boast, as he always does when there is fog in nearby

Northeast Harbor, that when the Jesuits were blacked out the sun was probably shining brilliantly in Bar Harbor.)

When the weather cleared, the *Jonas* came in past the cliffs and anchored, it is believed, in Cromwell Harbor.

The Jesuits had hardly reached shore, planted their cross and named the spot St. Sauveur when smoke signals were seen and Indians appeared. They implored the Jesuits to sail around to their side of the island where, they said, Asticou, their sagamore, was mortally ill and craved baptism to save his soul from perdition.

No Jesuit could resist such a plea and they were paddled along the cliffs to what now is called Manchester's Point, near the entrance to Somes Sound. There they found Asticou suffering from nothing more than a cold in the head. But the ruse brought satisfaction to all, particularly, it may be assumed, to the precocious Indian real estate promoters. Father Pierre Biard, professor of theology at Lyons

Hull's Cove.

and spiritual leader of the expedition, enthusiastically approved a new site across the way at Fernald's Point. Asticou was baptized; the Jesuits raised their cross a second time and on the same day brought the *Jonas* around and transferred the name St. Sauveur.

Father Biard wrote of the location:

"A beautiful hillside sloping gently from the seashore . . . twenty-five or thirty acres. . . . The harbor smooth as a pond, being shut in by the large island of Mount Desert, the sides sheltered by certain smaller islands which break the force of the wind and waves and fortify the entrance. It is large enough to hold any fleet of ships and can discharge within a cable's length of the shore."

Bald-pated, black-robed priests went diligently about the task of converting the heathen, but soon dissension arose. Some of the leaders pressed for immediate fortification of the settlement, but unfortunately the Sieur de la Saussaye, chief of the colony, had his way and agriculture was given first priority.

So when Argall arrived in the ship *Treasurer* from Jamestown, Virginia, the

Here come watery wayfarers for a face lifting . . boat yard at Hull's Cove.

colonists were utterly without defense. Some Indians fishing off the outer islands innocently told Argall of the settlement. When they realized the English were enemies, it was too late. One of the unhappy red men was compelled to act as pilot and the *Treasurer* came boiling up the Western Way, bunting snapping in the breeze, guns blazing and drums and trumpets sounding furiously.

The *Jonas* swung helplessly at anchor, her canvas rigged as awnings against the sun.

A prayer by young Father Gilbert du Thet, voiced before leaving France, that he might die in the service of God in America, was soon answered. Others were too stunned to act, but seized a match and touched off the *Jonas'* cannon. Unhappily, the young padre, more familiar with his paternosters than with the duties of a gunner's mate, neglected to aim and no damage was done. He fell before the next volley from the *Treasurer* and was buried at the foot of the cross so recently raised ashore.

The French fled, some into the forest, some up the cliffs, of the mountain now called St. Sauveur. Prodded by hunger, they soon returned to become prisoners. Argall took the majority, including Father Biard, and the *Jonas* back to Virginia. A few, permitted to depart in an open boat, reached Nova Scotia.

Argall returned some time later to complete the demolition of St. Sauveur, and Father Biard accompanied him, an act many thought came close to treason. Eventually all the survivors of the colony returned to France, Father Biard presumably to his placid theology chair at Lyons.

Some historians have painted Sir Samuel Argall as something of a monster, contending he was unnecessaarily cruel and ruthless, but in cold analysis, he probably was no more vengeful than many of his contemporaries. Certainly he came to Mount Desert under orders to evict trespassers on territory claimed by his king.

Argall made secure a niche in history when he kidnapped Pocahontas in 1612, as a hostage to enforce return of English prisoners held by Powhatan. For this deed, he was roundly berated in some quarters, particularly by the sentimental. But the strategem was successful and Argall might seem a greater scoundrel had not the dusky princess enjoyed her captivity so well that she declined to return to the family tepee when the prisoners were liberated.

Cadillac and Madame de Gregoire

T HE imprint of Antoine de la Mothe Cadillac was not very deep, but so indelible it still serves as basis for land titles on Mount Desert.

Louis XIV, anxious to have his subjects quit roaming the forests and establish French feudalism in the New World, granted the island to Cadillac in 1688 as part of the seigneurie of Douaquet.*

Cadillac's residency was fleeting and ineffectual, but much later it helped a granddaughter, Mme. Marie Therese de Gregoire, win recognition by the Massachusetts legislature of her claim to the island.

Like Champlain, Cadillac was well educated, a skilled navigator and cartographer, and eager to futher the interests of the French crown. But there the similarity ended.

His vanity prompted him to appropriate a high-sounding but synthetic title; his self-interest made him rich. A brawler and a persuasive and colorful letter-writer, in his own behalf, some suspected he inspired Rostand's Cyrano de Bergerac. Unlike Champlain, he could not abide priests and Jesuits, but like his predecessor of eighty-four years, he left very practical sailing directions for sea lanes around Mount Desert. He was, despite his faults, or perhaps because of them, a very able and effective administrator, although he did not have time to display those talents on the island.

One of his more enthusiastic reports, to the Ministry of Marine, probably caused the French to make this a staging area for adventures against the British.

*According to the account of Sir Edmund Andros, Governor of New England who sailed down from Boston in 1688, Cadillac and his wife were living on the eastern side of the island, probably near Schooner Head, Bar Harbor.

Here they readied warships for action and rendezvoused with their Indian allies. The report stated:

"This is an island which is twelve leagues in circumference, and is very high and mountainous. It also serves as an excellent landmark for ships from Europe, bound either for Port Royal or Boston. The harbor of Monts Deserts or Monts Coupes is very good and very beautiful. There is no sea inside, and vessels lie, as it were, in a box. There are four entrances. The northeast one is the best; it has nine fathoms of water. Good masts may be got here and the English formerly used to come here for them. Four leagues southeast of Monts Deserts, there is a rock [Mount Desert Rock] which is not covered at high water."

Cadillac brought his Quebec bride to Mount Desert and their eldest daughter may have been born there. Whatever his plans for the island, they were not carried out because he was recalled by new wars. After winning the confidence of Canadian Governor Frontenac, Cadillac founded the trading post that became the robust city of Detroit. There he spent six years climbing the ladder of wealth and influence and signing official papers as "Seigneur de Douaquet et Monts Deserts." He was associated with lands which became eight states of the Union and served as governor of Louisiana. His career suffered at least one unpleasant interruption — a brief sojourn in the Bastile.

Of all the French sea fighters who gathered at Mount Desert and gave Frenchman Bay its name, Pierre la Moyne d'Iberville was far and away the most daring and picturesque. His exploits make fiction seem wan and pale. D'Iberville and one of his numerous brothers, all of whom carried the banner of courage high, burned Syracuse, New York, in 1690, and a few years earlier fell upon the English at Hudson's Bay, taking two forts and three ships. D'Iberville also discovered the mouth of the Mississippi.

At Mount Desert, d'Iberville and his reckless associates waited in ambush behind the Porcupines in their fast vessels for passing English shipping, then swooped down like osprey on unwary herring.

Mme. de Gregoire as a child in France listened to stories of the exploits of her adventurous grand-pere, but it was not until she reached middle age that she thought she might repair fallen family fortunes by laying claim to the Cadillac grant.

With adroit feminine power she persuaded a group of important dignitaries, the Marquis de Lafayette, and Monsieur Otto, French Ambassador to the United States, Thomas Jefferson and Benjamin Franklin, that at least half the island should be hers.

The Massachusetts legislature at the time felt very kindly toward la belle France because of aid furnished in the Revolution, so when her daughter appeared in the role of suppliant, m'sieur, what could it do? It promptly performed a few legislative gymnastics and found Mme. de Gregoire held title to whatever land Massachusetts owned on Mount Desert. Citizenship for Mme. de Gregoire, her husband, Barthelemy, and their three children was thrown in for good measure, although it appears they never took the trouble to learn English.

The de Gregoires, who blithely entertained a delusion they could reside in

Southwest Harbor Views: "The Back Shore"; A Manset pier; through Manset birches; Norwood Cove.

pleasant circumstances in Boston on gains from the grant, arrived at Mount Desert in 1788, exactly a century after Cadillac's visit. Woefully ill-equipped for a life of pioneering, they built a rough dwelling and mill at Hull's Cove and attempted farming.

The settlers already established on Mount Desert, with solid squatters' rights, were not unduly impressed by the de Gregoires or their legal papers. They were courteous and polite and some paid the five dollars in "milled gold dollars" required for a de Gregoire title, but land was worth just about what was put into it by brains and brawn.

They also were amused by Mme. de Gregoire's attempt to entertain Indians at her home, an obvious effort to support the tradition of pleasant relationships between Grand-pere Cadillac and the red men.

Mme. de Gregoire had been a trifle tardy in claiming the island, for the legislature shortly before her arrival granted the western half to John Bernard, son of Sir Francis Bernard, last Tory governor at Boston. John benefited little from the grant and it is doubtful if the de Gregoires would have fared much better had they gained title to the entire island.

Fall of their land holdings was precipitous. Their 104,275 acres melted rapidly in measurement and value and in nine years tax valuation of their property fell from $1,845 to $633. In 1806, the de Gregoires deeded the remnants of the grant to Royal Gurley, who supported the parents until their deaths, M. de Gregoire in 1810 and Mme. de Gregoire the next year. Their three children vanished from the scene, presumably returning to France.

For some years, only a wooden cross marked the de Gregoire gravestone in Hull's Cove; the final remembrance of the name hereabouts, the cosy apartment-hotel, the De Gregoire, which stood at the junction of Eden and West Streets, built about the turn of the last century, is no more. It was levelled like a tinder box just before the Great Fire was diverted on its march toward the town on October 23, 1947.

But the de Gregoire grant still has legal standing at the Hancock County courthouse and the eastern side of Mount Desert is the only place in the United States except Louisiana where all land titles must be traced back to the French crown.

The Wreck of the Grand Design

IN 1739 occurred the island's most famous shipwreck. The *Grand Design*, a sailing vessel of almost 300 tons, bound for Pennsylvania from Ireland with a company of some two hundred persons of wealth and importance, together with bond servants and a cargo of fine Irish linen, was driven off her course by a series of wild autumn gales climaxed by an even fiercer storm which drove her high upon the pink granite slabs of Long Ledge, at the entrance to tiny Ship Harbor.

So high aground was the *Grand Design* hurled that those aboard were able to walk ashore. It was nearly thirty years before the arrival of the first settler and they were on the most remote and desolate side of the island. When December came and no aid arrived, the captain and one hundred unmarried men put out through the snow drifts to cross the island. None was ever seen again.

A red flannel petticoat flown above the highest rock as a distress signal attracted no attention, for no coasting vessels traveled that way in the winter. The food supply dwindled rapidly and a rigorous winter prevented replenishments. Deaths became more frequent.

Indians who could not be made to understand the plight of the survivors, or their need for assistance, exchanged dried venison for bolts of linen, then stole some of their much needed tools and utensils.

Later other Indians arrived, including one who understood English who made good a promise to deliver a letter. Eventually a vessel arrived from Warren, but the rescuers found only a few survivors shivering in remnants of their rich wardrobes and draped in yards of trailing linen. Earlier the bond servants had been freed that they might have equal opportunity to survive, but this gesture served little practical purpose.

Ship Harbor at low tide. This placid mirror close by Bass Harbor Head, surrounded by spruces and pink granite, is named for an incident in the War of 1812: an English raider, seeking to escape a pursuing Yankee ship, ran through the tricky entrance, and grounded, its crew taking to the woods.

There is reason to believe that descendants of some of the *Grand Design's* survivors reside in Maine. Two young widows married Warren men and they are known to have reared families.

More than a century and a half after the shipwreck, boys playing along the

Seawall at the edge of Manset near Southwest Harbor. Not far away occurred island's famous 1739 shipwreck when the *Grand Design* piled against the rocky shore of Long Ledge near Wonderland. Its load of passengers from Ireland nearly all perished on the then remote coast.

Seawall shore were discovered "skipping" into the sea corroded coins dated from 1720 to 1730. Perhaps they unearthed the cache of a wealthy passenger who died without revealing its location.

Mount Desert has known, one hundred and fifty years later, at least three other notable, but not so tragic shipwrecks. A granite-laden vessel sank at the Hall Quarry loading wharf and slid off into such deep water in Somes Sound that not even her topmasts were visible. A coal carrier was wrecked near the location of the *Grand Design's* end, but she brought windfall to the islanders, who were in urgent need of fuel at the time. Still another vessel, laden with grindstones, came to grief in the same locality, furnishing islanders with knife and axe sharpeners for many years. Some unsalvaged grindstones are visible through the clear water off Northeast Harbor.

The Bernard Grant

S IR Francis Bernard was among the several who at one time or another held title to the entire island of Mount Desert, and like the others was unable to do much about it. Another Englishman, Sir Thomas Mansell, a Vice Admiral in His Majesty's Navy, one hundred and fifty years before, had bought the island from the crown for one hundred and ten pounds and the privilege of naming it Mount Mansell, but the Admiral did nothing about settlement and his claim went by default.*

Sir Francis was the last colonial governor at Boston. A meticulous administrator, he was none too tactful with the colonists, but he had used his own funds lavishly to beautify the facade of the old State House and to assist Harvard College; the General Court of Massachusetts, of which Maine was then a part, believed that he was entitled to consideration.

At about that time, in fact for some years succeeding 1760, a landowner felt he needed at least a hundred acres in which to take a full swing at destiny. Even at that date this type of real estate parcel was becoming scarce around Boston and other populous coastal centers; the cry was not go West, but go Down East, young man.

The grandeur of Sir Francis' way of life had been so out of tune with his

*Manset, between Southwest Harbor and the open ocean at Seawall, one of the most enchanting spots on the island, gets its name from a distortion of Mansell. An island post office clerk of the past, no doubt scratching with a mutilated post office pen, inadvertently crossed the two ll's; eventual result down the years was Manset. The U.S. Department of Interior, however, two hundred years later, put the Mount Mansell name back on the island map, affixing it to one of the eastern peaks of the Western Mountains when they became part of Acadia National Park.

resources that the picture of grabbing off Mount Desert Island had a compelling appeal. The nobleman was a brilliant lawyer and a respected administrator; he liked the good life in the governor's great mansion on the shore of Jamaica Pond; on Sundays he favored the church where the sermon was the briefest.

He petitioned for the opportunity of a grant of the island in 1762 and eagerly accepted the conditions that he survey and settle it.

Hundreds already had preceded him Down East in anything that could float, lured by fine free lands, well timbered, with unequaled harbors, waters, fresh and salt full of fish, with game of wide variety and streams ready to turn the wheels of grist and saw mills.

Sir Francis, with his retinue, traveled with befitting pomp and ceremony in the revenue cutter *Cygnet*, anchoring off what now is Southwest Harbor.

Much earlier, Captain John Smith, who had little patience with weaklings, caustically remarked that anyone who starved in Maine deserved that fate. One of the *Cygnet's* officers must have shared the opinion as he listed Mount Desert's resources.

"Its natural production," he recorded, "are oak, beech, maple and all sorts of spruce and pines . . . ash, poplar, birch of all sorts, white cedar, sassafras and many other sorts of wood, we know no name for a great variety of shrubs, among which is the filbert. Fruits such as raspberrys, strawberrys, cranberrys, gooseberrys and currants. It has all sorts of soil. . . . Its inhabitants of the brute creation are moose, deer, bear, fox, wolf, otter, beaver, martins, wild cat and many other animals of the fur kind, all kinds of wild fowl, hares, partridges brown and black . . . codfish is ever taken in any quantitys with very convenient beaches for drying and curing them. Shellfish of all sorts . . . fine prawns and shrimps . . . there are great quantitys of pease sufficient to feed innumerable number of herds and cattle, a great quantity of cherries."

He also noted the "extraordinary fine harbor . . . the best anchoring ground in the world."

While the governor was rowed up a "river," actually Somes Sound, his

View of The Marsh . . . winter terrain such as faced the hundred lost men of the *Grand Design* . . . Marker at left divides Southwest Harbor from Tremont.

Bass Harbor ... from Bernard.

surveyors went about the task of measuring his new domain. At the head of the Sound, he found two settlers who had preceded him, Abraham Somes and James Richardson. Bernard decided to permit them to remain and gave them deeds inscribed on birch bark.

He regarded the Somes dwelling as "rather unfinished," but noted the codfish drying outside and the "artificialness" of a nearby beaver dam. He also was impressed by the "notable" Mrs. Somes and her four pretty daughters.

Bernard learned that two other families were squatters on Cranberry Island, evidence that already the principles of no settlement without survey were breaking down.

After a week's visit, during which he sustained himself sumptuously on game his gunners brought in, the sybaritic Oxford graduate, having written a Latin poem about his new lands, returned to Boston. He sailed in the *Cygnet* as far as Portsmouth, where he was met on shore by his lady with their "chariot."

Patriot uprisings brought his plans for developing and exploiting Mount Desert to an abrupt end. An overzealous servant of his king, Bernard had won the enmity of Sam Adams and he was recalled to England in 1776 and kicked upward to a baronetcy. As his ship cleared Boston Harbor, the patriots gleefully rang bells and fired cannon to speed his departure.

Before Bernard died in 1779, he willed the island to his son, John, a resident of Bath, Maine. But meanwhile, all his estates had been confiscated by the victorious colonials, and John had much difficulty gaining recognition for his claim.

Eventually young Bernard satisfied the Massachusetts legislature he had been a Yankee sympathizer and it granted him half of the island: he promptly mortgaged half of that, hastened back to England, and like his father, became a baronet, forgetting Mount Desert for all time.

Now only the family name remains, serving a small fishing and shipbuilding settlement on Bass Harbor.

The Early Settlers

Mount Desert slumbered in primeval grandeur more than a century and a half after Champlain's discovery before the island knew its first permanent settler.

Desultory attempts at colonization and visits by men on warlike missions intervened, but it remained for Abraham Somes, sailing up from Gloucester for a cargo of staves, in 1761, to resolve that here his home should be. Somes returned the following year with his wife and four daughters and with his axe hewed out their log dwelling.

The site now is known as Somes' Point, at the head of Somes Sound, which with Somesville, owes its name to the first settler.

The second was James Richardson. He and his wife and five children arrived the same year, also from Gloucester, and settled at Richardson's Cove.

In a letter dated April 20, 1816, Somes related that firewater was the currency of the times in dealing with the Indians.

"I mean now," he wrote, "to give you a history of my discovering the Island of Mount Desert, where in the year 1775 the Indians were the only owners of the soil. I was in a Chebacco boat and one Eben Sutton of Ipswich in another. . . . We were boarded by a number of savages. . . . I asked how much occopy [spirits] I must give him [the chief] for that island [Greenings]. He answered, 'Oh, a great deal. A whole gallon.'

"Then the said Sutton asked the chief how much for that island, pointing to an island [Suttons] lying to the Eastward. The Governor [chief] said two quarts. We paid them in rum. He took a piece of birchbark and described the same to us

25

but we not understanding, neither the description nor the worth of the islands never attended to the subject nor took care of the birchbark and left them to drink and to take the good of their bargain." In later years, authorities recognized such Indian documents.

The earliest settlers raised their cabins on shore sites, near streams which would be used for waterpower and close to grass and marsh land for grazing livestock. Nearby islands . . . the Cranberries (Big Island and Little Island, as the year round residents call them) and Bartlett . . . appealed to some because of their proximity to good fishing, the land was less densely forested and the shores were piled with driftwood, a convenient fuel supply and not considered in those days for its decorative value. Lobsters could be gathered amongst the rocks but were then not much esteemed as food. The deep freeze had its precursor; when a "beef critter" was killed, part of it was salted, but the rest was kept frozen and hung outdoors to be used fresh throughout the winter.

The western side of Mount Desert was favored by the pioneers because it was nearest to the route of coasting vessels. Later the trend was toward the more fertile eastern shore on Frenchman Bay where richer meadows meant fat cattle; an added inducement was the ease in obtaining titles in the de Gregoire area.

From the start, there was a dependence on worship. Now throughout the island there are churches of many faiths, but in the early days religion wore an austere face and was hard to come by. We have the instance of a husband and wife who applied for church membership. The sister could be accepted, they were told, "but the brother would have to stand awhile."

After churches were established, Sunday morning sermons often lasted hours with more services in the afternoon. Records of Eden Church speak of a young lady who had explored associations beyond the parish. She was reinstated upon her promise never again to attend a quilting bee.

A Somesville man met the fee of the minister who married him with fifty cents and a quarter of veal.

Island churches were unheated until the 1850's and many ministers in winter wore greatcoats and mittens in the pulpit while worshipers clad in similar array shivered in the pews. Some of the members did not forswear the warmth of a nearby grog shop during intermissions.

The ruggedness of early life on the island is indicated by a vote in 1790 to pay bounties on bear, wildcat and wolves. Bullet molds were an essential of each hunting kit as was the spoon mold in the home. But marauding animals were not all that plagued the settlers. They were forced to call for assistance from the authorities in Boston to cope with trespassers from the mainland who too frequently helped themselves to hay already cut and dried. Colonel Thomas Goldthwaite duly arrived and rendered the proper aid.

Eden, now Bar Harbor, was incorporated as a separate unit in 1796 and Paul Dudley Sargent called voters to assemble at Captain Samuel Hull's house at Hull's Cove on April 4th of that year. There some curious but then realistic offices were created. There were no corpse viewers such as the island of Nantucket of similar

"Ey-ah (or Yep) . . . looks like a goo-ud summer" . . . Bernard citizen prognosticates.

era provided, but there were fence viewers and Daniel Rodick and Daniel Richardson were the first appointees. Other Eden roles were colorful; surveyors of shingles were Ebenezer Salisbury, David Hamor and Thomas Wasgatt; surveyor of staves was Henry Knowles; sealer of leather was Elkanah Young; culler of fish, Timothy Smallidge; hog reeve, Stephen Salisbury; poundkeepers, Joseph Mayo and Ebenezer Salisbury; field drivers, Joseph Mayo and Solomon Higgins and tythingmen were Ebenezer Salisbury and Moses Wasgatt. The titles have passed into obscurity but the names of the first settlers remain: the Lelands, Higgins and Rodicks still serve the community through other avenues. The role of moderator and selectmen continue.

Free speech always has been the governing rule of Mount Desert town meetings and there the smallest taxpayer is entitled to as loud and long a voice as the largest. It is not a gag rule per se but on the other hand, probably no accident that Bar Harbor town meetings are held in March. Then summer residents are back in the city worrying about income taxes, or at winter resorts.

Shipbuilding early became an important Mount Desert industry, although vessels were limited in size to about 100 tons — never as large as the brig *Pilgrim*, built at Stave Island, across Frenchman Bay, and immortalized in Richard Henry Dana's *Two Years Before the Mast*.

Sails that propelled some of the vessels built at Norwood's Cove, Southwest

There is something strictly New England about fan windows. When horseshoes were incorporated, they usually were up-turned, to retain the luck supposedly attached. This oak-ribbed structure, despite the inverted horseshoe, survived the great fire of 1947 as did all of Salisbury Cove. In the old days, fan windows were like a signature, never copied or counterfeited.

Harbor, were made of linen Mary Hadlock Manchester wove from flax she grew nearby.

Much of the early shipbuilding was concentrated at the Pool, on Cranberry Island, and launchings always were gala occasions usually ending with a dinner and celebration dance. Characteristic is this item from a diary which tells of a launching at Pretty Marsh and of a relative who went on a few days ahead to assist the family in preparation for the country dinner which consisted of "beans, brown bread baked in a brick oven, boiled ham, vegetables, and condiments galore, Indian pudding, pumpkin pie and doughnuts."

A Salisbury Cove shipbuilder, who could not forget the beauty of the lines of vessels he sent down his ways, erected this as his dwelling. He sacrificed a second story to retain the roof line. The unusual upper low windows provided ventilation. Old seafarer's home now is part of Mount Desert Biological Laboratory.

One house raising is worth recording, that of Jonah Corson and his wife, Martha, at Southwest Harbor, about 1830. When the foundation was ready, friends and neighbors worked with such zeal that the house was erected in a day. After a bounteous supper and many toasts, a seafaring guest mounted the ridgepole and declaimed:

> 'Here's to Jonah's industry and Martha's delight,
> Framed in a day and raised before night."

Then he christened the new dwelling in nautical style by smashing a bottle of rum on the roof.

Many skilled shipbuilders still dwell on Mount Desert and are employed in the six well-equipped yards. The more facile carpenters have always been attracted to shipbuilding; and for good reason, yacht carpentering pays the better money.

The oath of Hippocrates seldom carried heavier responsibility than on the island in early days. Dr. Kendall Kittredge arrived about 1799 and his weathered saddlebags, which may be seen in the Mount Desert Museum at Somesville, testify to the medico's struggles with the elements to reach his scattered patients. Blue Hill and Surry bonfires occasionally summoned Kittredge. After crossing the wide bay, the doctor would find a good neighbor waiting on the shore to direct him to his patient. Before Dr. Kittredge, islanders were forced to rely on the natural skills of Grandma'am Baker in time of illness, who was often carried in a handbarrow across ice and rough country.

Dr. William Spear arrived in Tremont in 1846 and practiced more than half a century. Sometimes when visting patients on the islands he was forced to lie on the bottom of leaky boats, reaching his destination with clothing frozen to the planks.

Rich's piety precipitated his wife's taunts. "When I die, I'll wear a Heavenly crown" he insisted. The prophecy appears dimly on gravestone, located between Tremont and Bernard. (Right) Manset family burial ground, typical of many on the Island.

British War Raiders

DURING the Revolution and War of 1812 settlers were harassed by Britishers. In 1775 a boatload of soldiers came ashore and raided the John Manchester cabin at the mouth of Somes Sound while the owner was hunting. They drove his oxen and cows onto the beach, killed and quartered them and took even the hides back to their ship, as well as potatoes and other stores set aside for the winter. They even destroyed Manchester's cooking utensils, saying "they could starve."

Later a moose came out of the woods and started swimming across the Sound. Manchester and his wife followed — she with a paddle and he with his flintlock to make the kill. With milk from a young cow that had strayed, and moose meat, fish and clams, they survived the winter.

In the War of 1812 some settlers had to pay tribute lest their properties were destroyed.

Rather than have his vessel burned on the ways Captain Amariah Leland gave up $500 in gold. William Mason and Thomas Paine, fishing in a small boat in Frenchman Bay, were wounded by the crew of an English barge; Mason died next day in a house on Bar Island. William Wasgatt, Elisha Young and William Thompson were carried to Halifax and England and confined in prison until the war closed.

In August, 1814, the *Tenedos,* a British sloop of war, anchored between Bear and Sutton islands. Captain Benjamin Spurling knew what to expect and had two of his vessels run up at high tide from Norwood's Cove into Harmon's Brook, Southwest Harbor, where he camouflaged their topmasts with green trees. Then

Spring and fall in Somesville: Apple blossoms at the head of the Sound . . . Old Meeting House: a Christopher Wren design whose odd double aisles make weddings hazardous.

he rowed over to the ship and offered a yoke of slaughtered oxen if the British would forego their purpose. The English invited him forcibly to "go with them, and see the vessels burn."

From the shore one very able patriot set out in a small boat to row to Castine for a supply of ammunition. Rallying word was passed along by swift-footed runners and horseback riders as far as to Colonel Black in Ellsworth, but the men of Eden and Ellsworth arrived too late to participate. The dawn engagement was well handled by the Southwest Harbor contingent.

Crowding their hostage Captain Spurling underfoot, two barges carrying about a hundred Britishers headed toward shore. The local militia, well hidden behind thickets and resting their weapons comfortably on boulders, opened fire. The reply from the barge's pivot gun went wild, breaking branches, hitting rocks, but wounding no one. Later two boys, who had gone aboard the *Tenedos* to sell raspberries, saw seven bodies lowered into the hold. Samuel Hadlock of Little Cranberry had two fingers grazed by a bullet — the only damage on the American side. Captain Spurling was released and the *Tenedos* sailed out of the harbor.

The Spurlings, who came from the western side of the island were of rugged stock. In 1818, Captain Samuel, master of the schooner *Cashier,* trounced a pirate ship off Trinidad and was presented by grateful Cubans with a sword and a brace of pistols. Asked by home folks how he did it, all he could offer was, "gave them a little bit of Hell, Maine style."

Even beautiful little Ship Harbor which is in the National Park lands near Bass Harbor Head, has a historical legend. One windy autumn day a British privateer was being chased across Blue Hill Bay by an irate Yankee ship; the raider seeking to escape to sea through the passage between Bass Harbor Head, and Gott Island found the way blocked by an oncoming American fishing smack. The trapped privateer then ran for the tricky entrance of an adjacent punch-bowl harbor at Long Ledge — a pink granite peninsula that in former years caught the

32

Kelp at Weaver's Ledge near Wonderland.

Low tide at Ship Harbor, now within National Park land near Bass Harbor and lying between Seawall and McKinley. . . . The town line passes through the center dividing Southwest Harbor, left, from Tremont, right.

wreck of the *Grand Design* — squirmed inside and grounded. The crew waded ashore and took to the woods. In time the privateer broke up and legend has it that she went to the bottom and that her timbers were visible in the clear water for years afterward.

The First Rusticators

THE earliest summer visitor of record arrived September 1844, Thomas Cole, forerunner of the Hudson River School of Painting, took eight days to reach the island travelling overland from Castine. Frederick Church, Thomas Birch and later William Morris Hunt, all eventually museum names, followed him to Mount Desert and produced such compositions as Eagle Lake, the Beehive, Echo Lake and the Porcupine Islands.

Thomas Cole named Eagle Lake for the bald eagles which soared over his easel. He once said, with a demonstration of superior hearing: "One might easily fancy himself in the forests of the Alleghanies, but for the dull roar of the ocean breaking the stillness." The ocean is a full three miles from Eagle Lake.

A. D. Bache, scientist, who made some surveys at mid-century from the top of Cadillac (then Green Mountain), stimulated the visits of Professor Nathaniel Shaler, the Harvard geologist. In 1853, a crude survey station appeared on top of the highest mountain.

Then, in 1858, Robert Carter, Washington correspondent of the New York Tribune, wrote of a voyage from Boston to Bar Harbor, for fun and research in marine zoology. It contained his opinions of the earliest rusticators.

After 1870, steamers began to call at the Southwest Harbor dock and in later years they entered Frenchman Bay. "Mealers and hauled mealers," tired of hotels and boarding houses, wanted places of their own. Apheus Hardy of Boston, who bought Birch Point in 1867, became Bar Harbor's first long-term summer visitor.

Rowboats appeared on Eagle Lake, a trail was cut through to Jordan Pond, where two men "in a short day's fishing, caught 500 trout." On July 4, 1874, a

Spring-fed Eagle Lake, source of Bar Harbor's supply of drinking water.

seventeen-piece band helped celebrate the turning on of the Eagle Lake water supply.

Meanwhile, as historian George Street observed, the summer residents helped "in support of the churches; they raised the standards of living and they introduced some undesirable luxuries, emphasized some unfortunate class distinctions, and were responsible for some vices formerly unknown, on the

West side of the Island near so-called Richtown . . . topographically another world . . . Open sea and abandoned motorboat cradle. Marshland brook, haunt of the wild duck, near West Tremont.

whole their influence was healthy to matters sanitary and social and religious."

Gradually the cottagers came into possession of the most desirable shore sites and more and more they surrounded themselves with the comforts of life. The island had a new industry — taxation. If you came to play, you had to pay.

But Southwest Harbor and Somesville, once called "Betwixt the Hills," the oldest parts of the island, continued their modest ways.

Northeast Harbor, perhaps with Seal Harbor the most substantial summer communities on the island, followed Bar Harbor's growth by about ten years.

In 1880 a company of Harvard students, calling themselves the Champlain Society, under Charles W. Eliot, Jr., camped on the eastern shore of Somes Sound and for two summers pursued scientific studies.

In 1882, the society moved to the head of Northeast Harbor. Young Eliot advised his father, President of Harvard, to locate between "Somes Sound and Seal Harbor — a site with beautiful views of the sea and hills, good anchorage, fine rocks and beach and no flats." President and Mrs. Eliot, guided to the spot by Squire Kimball, built at Asticou Hill.

It was also the same year that Bishop Doane of Albany came to board at Squire Kimballs'. The Bishop was charmed by the local people. "He mentioned their fresh and original way of putting things which have a zest of real raciness to their talk, and they were kind and cordial in their attitude to us who came from the outside."

In the early 1860's James Clement and brother-in-law E. T. Lyman, fishermen, were living at Seal Harbor. At Jordan's Pond, two lumbermen, G. W. Jordan and J. S. Jordan, had a more or less permanent camp. A rough trail for hauling logs ran from the pond to the beach at Seal Harbor, but the fire of 1864 swept the southern slopes of the hills, burning not only the standing timber but

Mount Desert has many waterfalls. Here is one, fed by recent rains, tumbling down the side of the Cadillac Mountain Drive. (Right) The "Eyre" . . . John D. Rockefeller, Jr.'s cottage at Seal Harbor, razed in 1964.

the soil, damage that cannot be seen today. For a time the beach and the hill area sold for a dollar an acre. Now Seal Harbor is the home of Rockefellers and Fords, and like individuals who also appreciate seclusion on their lofty sites — for which they paid more than a dollar per acre.

The 1870's — Bar Harbor's Early Vacationers

IN 1870, the first steamers to the island had begun calling at the dock in Southwest Harbor which was then as now the village on Mt. Desert most conversant with the open ocean.* Soon Bar Harbor would see four steamers a week. There were seven hotels in the town, most of them on Main Street. President U. S. Grant planned to extend his summer cruise to Bar Harbor, cancelled only when poor weather intervened. The resort had achieved a national reputation. In another year Bar Harbor had eleven hotels and was written up in *Harper's*.

Not all of these hostelries were of the Ritz variety. Nevertheless this first group of Bar Harbor hotels and boarding houses was novel, perhaps amusing, many including the "mealer" and "hauled mealer" variety of guests. An early guidebook, copyrighted by one Hugh Chisholm, declares that accommodations were rustic and simple.

> The rising bell rang at 6:30 and breakfast was served before seven. One complaining guest was answered, "Well, you came here for a change, didn't you? Now you've got it!" To another, sarcastically asking the boniface who taught him to keep a hotel, he retorted. "The Lord Almighty. . . . " A sophisticated New Yorker questioned what kind of griddle cakes were mentioned on the bill of fare. "Well, I call them fust rate," calmly said the table-girl. General complaints were made of fried meat supplied, and the housekeeper replied, "Fried fresh is good 'nuff for me and the cap'n, and I guess its good 'nuff for them starched-up city

---

*Why is Northeast Harbor so named? Because inhabitants of the earlier Southwest Harbor referred to their new neighbor as being "northeast of Southwest."

40

folk." Another metropolitan guest suggested, "Mr. Landlord, I shall put my boots outside my door tonight." And the hearty Innkeeper replied, "All right, sir, you'll find them there in the morning, we're all honest folk around here."

WEST END HOTEL   BAR HARBOR, ME.

Came the year 1874 and the town and its jury-built hotels ran into the same trouble that beset Zermatt, Switzerland in 1963. Typhoid! Overnight the Bay View House was evacuated while Henry Swift versified the situation.

"One night, when laugh and gay reply abound,
And loud with mirth the Bay View's walls resounded,
The doctors, in muffled conversation,
But listeners keen, by anxious terror stirred,
The words of evil omen overheard.
Dark fell the cloud; concealment now was vain:
From lip to lip flew one wild word: 'The drain!'
No caution could the dread announcement stay,
That all must leave within another day.

What boots it now to bid them stop till morning,
The timorous boarders bide no second warning;
As robins that a cherry tree invade,
Upon a gun-shot rustle from the shade,
As rats that overrun the farmer's store,
By footsteps started scamper from the floor —
So madly rush the guests from hall and stair
In terror flee, and leave the mansion bare,
While those whose illness must their flight postpone,
In dreary comfort hold the house alone."

Historian Richard Walden Hale goes on to say that the 1874 trouble lay beyond the drains; eight cases of typhoid and five more broke out when rusticators returned to their out-of-state homes. The national press got hold of the story and Bar Harbor was on the spot; word had gone out that the place was fever-infested. A funny aspect of the situation was the case of the bedridden lady in one of the hotels who refused to be carried out to safety until she had been formally introduced to each one of her rescuers.

Bar Harbor defenders tried to prove that only one well was infected. But the challenge was met far more conclusively when the ship carpenters of Eden came to the rescue, adapting the idea of a Bar Harborite who had gained experience in the West with placer mining flumes: inexpensive wooden troughs for

THE LOUISBURG

M. L. BALCH, Proprietor.

Some Representative Guests of The Louisburg.

Alexander Moseley,
Otis Norcross,
Oliver W. Peabody,
Arthur Little,
Henry M. Whitney,
Samuel Johnson,
J. Arthur Beebe,
Charles F. Sprague,
Stephen G. Marston,
Frederic R. Coudert,
Henry F. Dimock,
Samuel D. Babcock,
Brayton Ives,
William P. St. John,
Dr. F. Fremont Smith,
William E. Dodge,
James Ross Todd,
Rev. D. A. F. Schauffler,

J. M. Cook,
E. S. Pike,
Theodore Havemeyer,
James Parrish,
D. O. Mills,
William S. Wells,
George G. Haven,
William P. Blackwell,
Judge Miles Beach,
Hon. J. L. M. Curry,
Hon. Roswell P. Flower,
C. W. Bergner,
Lawrence Turnure,
Judge William Putnam,
Hibbard Porter,
John W. Mackay,
George W. Armstrong,
Francis L. Stetson.

COTTAGES: By making early application to the manager, families can secure separate cottage conveniently near the Louisburg, with table board and service from the hotel. Address

J. ALBERT BUTLER, Manager
The Louisburg,
Bar Harbor, Me.

An advertisement from an island newspaper of the '80's gives a cross section of Bar Harbor's guests in the era of the large hotels.

transporting water. The work started in time to be ready for the next summer's visitors. Surface drainages were in some instances converted into cesspools or were fed into sewers and thence led into the ocean. The June 18th edition of the New York *Herald* told the world that all was well — "Drainage regulated

Undisturbed by time; the weather-beaten shingles of a lobsterman's hideaway at Otter Creek.

so as to Prevent All Possibility of Recurrence of Trouble — Delicious Drives, Mountain Walks and Scenery — Abundant Trout."

On the fourth of July next, a seventeen-piece band celebrated the turning on of Eagle Lake water, the same soft tap water — the "Eagle Lake Ale" — that the town of Bar Harbor enjoys today. And so the 1874 crisis was over, the resort was saved.

The Island House, Southwest Harbor.

The Rodick House.

In 1875 Daniel Rodick was once again to enlarge his Rodick House until in 1882 it could hold well over six hundred guests. The town had passed from a field to that of a full-fledged spa.* The breakwater at the entrance of the harbor was built; and a cog railroad up Green (now Cadillac) Mountain went into operation.

In the early eighties Bar Harbor was pursuing a cosmopolitan life. A local scribe explained,

> "Bar Harbor offers a variety of pleasures unsurpassed in any summer resort in the country. It is not alone to the wealthy that the doors of pleasure are opened. One may spend a long vacation here as cheaply as at any resort. The hotels regulate their rates to accommodate all classes, from $2.00 a day upwards. The mountain, sea, and valley scenery are open to all without price or payment. Driving is one of the popular forms of amusements, and within the past few years bicycling has supplanted it in large measures, that enjoyable pleasure among the young people. The buckboard is indigenous to the soil and nowhere in the world can such handsome vehicles of the make be seen."

The enterprising '80's were now in force.

*Society editors early fell into the habit of calling the town a "fashionable spa."

A view of Bar Harbor from the bay, probably mid-1880's. The hotels shown, from left to right, are the Newport, the Rockaway, and the Agamont. In the background can be seen the roof of the Rodick House and, on the summit of Cadillac Mountain, the Green Mountain House.

The Green Mountain Railway

AN island entrepreneur, a newcomer by the fascinating name of Clerque, who guided the destinies of the Mount Desert Fertilizer Company, believed a cog railway up Green (now Cadillac) Mountain would attract people who wanted to spend the night at a crude hotel on the summit to see the sun set and rise.

A fanfare of publicity launched the venture; the Bangor *Mining Journal* in 1883 compared the proposed line with the funicular of Mount Vesuvius and the Rigi. The new locomotive arrived in a schooner from Portland and fourteen horses hauled it to Eagle Lake, which lies below the mountain. The gauge was four-and-a-half feet*; wood lying along the roadside was a convenient source of fuel.

The railroad did well the first year, paying a six per cent dividend, the best in its lifetime. Buckboards were not only picturesque but enterprising competitors and the realistic and jealous Mr. Clerque went so far as to have the carriage road dynamited. Such measures only delayed the inevitable, however, and although the railroad continued operation for seven years, evil days arrived in one of the up-and-down cycles that plague all summer resorts. The transportation and land boom collapsed and the little engine no longer wheezed up the mountain. The supporting *Wauwinnet,* a tiny steamer that carried the passengers to the base of the mountain, was scuttled by the owners in the deep water of Eagle Lake after her boiler and other fittings had been removed.

*Although the rails have long since been removed, traces of the railway can still be located near a small turnout on Jordan Pond Road, two-thirds of a mile south of the junction with the Summit Road.

The Green Mountain railway (above) and the Green Mountain House (below).

A depleted Mr. Clerque took off on a world cruise; reports told of his making a business connection with the Shah of Persia.

But there was a new lease on life for the fussy little locomotive. In 1895 there had been an accident to the engine of the Mount Washington cog railway; someone remembered where there was another of the same gauge. The little Green Mountain locomotive of Maine was removed to the White Mountains of New Hampshire to puff for years under the name of Old Peppersass before coming to a tragic end.

On July 20, 1929, on a last trip before retirement, Old Peppersass charged uncontrolled down Mount Washington's steep slope, plunged from a trestle called Jacob's Ladder, into a ravine, and exploded. A photographer, intent upon making pictures, jumped too late and was killed. Souvenir collectors carried away most of the fragments of Old Peppersass, so-called because its upright boiler and stack were thought to resemble a bottle of pepper sauce.

47

The Gilded Age —
And Beyond

B AR Harbor, then in the Town of Eden, had by 1880 graduated from the "rusticator" stage and entered its most glamorous era. Soon a roster of summer residents read like a list cautiously compiled by the editors of Dunn & Bradstreet.

A correspondent of the New York *Herald*, returning after a few years absence wrote in his newspaper; "The old time camping out, the salt junk and hard tack, ring-for-a-boy and then-get-it-yourself existence at the hotels is over, and with it has gone into the past much of that delightful freedom whose memory will be preserved for a little in some novels and much longer in tradition."

As road and rail climbed up the mountain the social life in the town below was beginning to assume majestic proportions. The Boston *Traveler* of 1881 reported on Bar Harbor.

> "There is more dressiness now than at the opening of last season . . . natty blue suits giving way to yellowish flannel for young men and maids . . . of yachts vying with mackerel in the harbor and there being money in a toll road up Green Mountain . . . of the number of permanent boarders being greater than at similar times in the past years."

In 1882 came incandescence and communication. Few landlords could longer limit the number of candles used by guests. There was the case of the Bar Harbor hotel keeper who flew into a rage when a bridegroom cut tallow candles into small pieces to increase illumination for his wife. In addition to the coming of electric lights, five telephone circuits were in operation. Hale recounts that systems of additional bells were so arranged that calls could not be heard by others save in the

Summer visitors, indigenous to Maine, early 1880's.

case of several subscribers on the same circuit. One potpourri of listeners seemed hardly to represent the essence of a private line for "so it was that four hotels, a livery stable, Bee's Store, and Dr. Amory were linked together."

Almost every evening face-to-face gaiety confronted the smart summer set, as expressed by an issue of the island press of 1882, which included a heterogeneous style note as observed at a Rodick House dance; "some ladies ... in full ball dress . . . others in ordinary mountain or walking costume . . . ".

"The opening ball at the new music-hall of the Rodick was a grand success. The floor was thronged with dancing couples and the piazza was packed with gazers. This was undoubtedly the grand success of the season. As usual, the costumes were various, some ladies coming in full ball dress, others in ordinary evening dress and still others in ordinary mountain or walking costume. A good effect was obtained by white dresses and dark colored turbans, mottled, brown, blue or dark red. Among the men, dress coats were few, ordinary 'cut-a-ways' being most prominent. The prime movers of the affair were Messrs. Johnson of Philadelphia and Spencer of New York. The orchestra was heard to good advantage. The sides of the room were lined with matrons, chaperones and interested spectators, absorbed in watching the gay scene before them. . . . The floor was smooth as glass and exceedingly slippery but abundance of chalk enabled gliding soles to retain their hold upon the waxy planks."

The Casino Skating Rink was doing a land office business. It was reported to be the largest rink in New England just as the Rodick was the largest hotel.

Continues the Bar Harbor newspaper of 1882 —

Spirited Bar Harbor tennis party of the '80's.

"Tomorrow evening, the first polo match, for a set of colors, will take place at the skating rink, and as everybody among the cottage and hotel people are much interested, owing to the high standing in society of the members of the contending clubs, a great audience will probably witness the contest. A large number of seats have been reserved and the demand, is brisk thus early. The prices are the same, however, as usual, the management not making any extra charge for reserving seats, simply wishing to accommodate their patrons."

There was also creature comfort for the occasional warm summer day. To combat the frigid water which rings most of the island, a condition which has always dismayed the tourist and has caused many a would-be summer resident to prefer Cape Cod, bath houses were installed on the newly opened West Street. These were not far from the site of the present Bar Harbor Club and its enormous pool of aquamarine-colored sea water.

The year 1887 saw the coming of the all-Pullman Bar Harbor Express carrying escapees from the heat of Washington, Baltimore, Philadelphia, and New York. A rash of land and improvement companies was breaking out — about thirteen in all. Much of this was sheer gambling; the list of deceased corporations can still be found in the Secretary of State's office in the Capitol at Augusta. Bar Harbor was seeing many an important visitor. Richard Hale relates that President Harrison came to the Island to visit James G. Blaine. In the Sawtelle collection at Islesford (off Northeast and Seal Harbors) can still be seen one of the cigars handed out on that auspicious occasion, complete with commemoration wrapper.

The Malvern Hotel, Kebo Street, destroyed in the 1947 fire.

In this era some visitors felt that Bar Harbor hotels should upgrade their facilities. Former guests, tired of being "mealers" and "hauled mealers," sought better accommodations or places of their own. Erected about this time were the Belmont, and De Gregoire, keyed to satisfy the tastes of those who had graduated from the "rusticator stage." De Grasse Fox, who eloped with a Biddle of Philadelphia, built the larger Malvern Hotel near Talleyrand Corner in Bar Harbor.

Charles Dudley Warner, who featured the charms of Cape Breton Island in *Baddeck and That Sort of Thing*, said en route to Nova Scotia,

> "Bar Harbor has one of the most dainty and refined little hotels in the world, The Malvern. Anyone can stay there who is worth two millions of dollars, or can produce a certificate from the recorder of New York that he is a direct descendant of Hendrick Hudson or Diedrich Knickerbocker."

At the threshold of the nineties Bar Harbor had become a social capital of the United States. There were those who bewailed the fashionable conquest and the change from fish and skeleton chickens at $5 the week, to reed birds, lobster, filet mignon and champagne at $5 a day, from "rocking" and mountain climbing to musicales and lawn parties.

A report on the town printed in the Bar Harbor *Record* declares that in 1896 echelons of rank were already in place.

> "The social life of the early 1880's was entirely different from that of today in Bar Harbor. Then it was a society without distinct dividing lines; it was hotel society life. The descendants of the hotel dwellers of those days are many of them 'cottagers' today. In hotel days the 'cottagers' met us on common ground. Today

the social life is but transferred from the cities with lines strictly drawn in circles. Still, to many, those were the days of happiest memory."

The pulse of Bar Harbor was indeed quickening.

As the pace accelerated the arteries felt the pressure. Observing that three new undertaking establishments had opened up in town, the *Herald* coyly remarked: "We trust that the presence of many physicians among our summer guests has not been misconstrued."

The Bangor *Commercial* of April, 1887, had a word about logistics: "The train arrangements this season will make it possible to go from New York to Bar Harbor in one day; thus making Mount Desert Island almost as accessible as Coney Island, while it is five times as comfortable." *Sic transit gloria . . .* now for freight only.

In 1887 a new carriage road was built up Cadillac, then called Green Mountain, a name that died hard even years after the Acadia National Park rechristened the summits within its domain. Activity was spinning furiously but with gyroscopic steadiness. The prevailing prices gave impetus to spending. It was a day when butter sold for twenty cents a pound; milk, eight cents a quart; twenty cents a dozen for the fattest of eggs. Corned beef was listed at seven cents a pound and round steak at twelve cents.

People were crowding to the Island. The Bar Harbor *Herald* of October 28, 1887, reports that, "The Maine Central carried to the Island the previous summer 15,192 passengers and carried away 15,759. The steamers carried approximately 10,500." (In 1977, the Island saw more than 3,000,000 visitors, but this number included tourists present for a day or two only.)

The Maine Central wharf, about 1910.

The Development of Kebo Valley

In 1887 an undaunted group of men of means formed the Acadia Park Company to develop real estate holdings on the meadowland below Cadillac and adjacent to the smaller Kebo Mountain, which today holds the "inner nine" fairways of the present Kebo Valley Golf Club. Two of the incorporators, Charles T. How of Bar Harbor and De Grasse Fox of Philadelphia, real estate promoters, in connection with Ogden Codman of Lincoln, Massachusetts, formed the Kebo Club's first charter on April 27th, 1888. Their incorporation, granted by the state of Maine, gave them permission to carry on in effect a giant subdivision. The official transaction states:

> "The business of purchasing and leasing real estate and erecting buildings and otherwise putting the property in suitable condition for the promotion and cultivation of athletic sports and furnishing innocent amusement for the public for reasonable compensation, including the erection and maintenance of a Casino which may include conveniences for dramatic and theatrical and musical entertainments under the name of Kebo Valley Club of Bar Harbor, Maine."

The year Kebo's articles of incorporation were signed, 1888, a little volume titled *Chisholm's Mt. Desert Guide* hit the Bar Harbor book shops. A chapter by M. F. Sweetser, called "Main Street," would seem to be a vivid picture of a vanished era.

> "Near the sidewalks stand the public carriages of the village, drawn up by scores: buckboards, single and double and quintuple, cut-unders, and barouches, with their drivers keenly vigilant for fares, and familiar with all the island roads. Here, also, are the private equipages of the cottagers, dog-carts, village-carts, tally-ho coaches, phaetons, chaises, road-wagons and ponderous and resplendent family carriages, with drivers and footmen in full livery, and a silvery rattling of harness chains. Equestrians, men and women and children, ride up and down the littered street; and here and there a wheelman pursues his solemn way.

> "In these equipages, and along the sidewalks and in the stores move the beauties of Belgravia and Vanity Fair, their trim and well-groomed appearance contrasting strangely with the unkempt surroundings. The young men, in their vivid-colored and striped blazers, or garments of white India silk, their bright-colored caps and Tam-o 'Shanters, tennis suits or yachting suits are hardly less resplendent than their sisters, the high-bred patrician girls, dressed like Parisiennes of the Faubourg St. Germain, in trim tailor-made suits, impressive in their apparent simplicity, or fairy-like in delicate summer gowns with marvelous pleatings, vests of India silk, panels of rich velvet, sprayings of lace, and shimmerings of white lawn."

An early view of Bar Harbor's Main Street.

Work began that same summer, 1888, on the Casino building, a part of which by another year was to become the clubhouse of the Kebo Valley Club. This dual activity by the two corporations, Acadia Park Company and Kebo, with the latter renting from the former, makes it difficult to pin down an actual starting date for the Kebo Valley club whose leased clubhouse quarters within the Casino building did not open until July 18, 1889. The structure, housing both Acadia Park Company and the Kebo Club, was located at the foot of the hill off the present third hole. Driveways came in from the Eagle Lake Road and as far away as the Cromwell Harbor Road where the eighteenth tee of today stands, the Edsel Ford Hole. All of Kebo's holes are now named for a celebrated member, each tee bearing a bronze name plaque set in an impressive block of stone.

A social note of the early nineties describes life within the Kebo Club:

"When it is remembered that there are upwards of one hundred and seventy-five cottages at Bar Harbor, occupied during the summer by their owners, the elite of society from Boston, New York, Philadelphia, Washington and other of our large cities, the visitor will be prepared for a great deal of gaiety. The Kebo Valley club House, a beautiful building erected in the midst of fine grounds near the Eagle Lake Road, is the center of amusement for the fashionables. In the building are a pretty little theater and a restaurant; and the grounds include a race track, golf ground, a baseball field, several tennis courts and croquet lawns. Most of the ladies and gentlemen who visit Bar Harbor belong to this Club. The club house was opened the 18th of July, 1889. During the season, the little theatre connected with the Club is the scene of many amateur performances, musicals, etc., and there is hardly a day during the season that the Club does not entertain some celebrity."

54

The Edsel Ford 18th Tee.

Kebo still had a long way to go before golf would make its appearance in 1892. In the beginning the horse had prominence. The Kebo Race Committee announced that the first annual race meeting would be held at the Kebo racetrack August 7, 1889 at 3:00 P.M. The initial event was a "hurdle race of one mile over five hurdles." The second race was a half mile dash for polo ponies not "over 14 hands" — for the Malvern Cup. There were two other races on the card. Pictures of the event show a spread of carriages and buckboards jammed around the track, and spectators crowded in and around the clubhouse. The horse was for four years

The Bar Harbor Horse Show, held at Robin Hood Park, today the site of the Jackson Laboratory.

to occupy first place, to share his glory only in 1891 when the "golf grounds" were laid out. By 1892 six holes had been built in and around the race track. Four years later a complete nine hole course had been finished with a yardage of 25,000 yards. *The Golfer* magazine of 1898 described the new golf links as one of the finest in the country.

Life at Kebo continued with a vibrant tenor. Golf, baseball, croquet, tennis, light theatricals and lively parties filled the summer days and nights.

The long Labor Day weekend, terminating for most socially minded Bar Harborites the intensive activity of the summer, is generally ushered out — even to the present day — with a fanfare of celebration. In 1890, on the last Saturday of August, Kebo staged an ambitious and imaginative horse gymkhana. The following Monday was set aside as an alternative in case of rain.

Programs of the extravaganza note that James W. Gerard, Jr., ambassador to Germany from 1913 to 1917, rode in every race wearing colors of pink. The card suggested that considerable ability (other than horsemanship) was essential, such as the saddling and girthing of one's pony, and the donning and doffing of waistcoats. Then to horse, the contestant making "the best of his way to the winning post."

Other events required the carrying of "manikins" astride the ponies — if manikin connoted a pretty girl this was probably a well-relished diversion. One dash stipulated the lighting of a cigar, then galloping to the line with an umbrella held aloft. A Potato and Bucket Race necessitated a special talent for balance and precision; the eighth and last contest required carrying an egg in a wooden spoon at full speed.

Bubble Pond, Acadia National Park.

The Gymkhana Races were open to horses of all ages and sizes. The advance bill is reprinted here in full:

KEBO VALLEY CLUB.

Gymkhana Races and other Events,

—ON—

SATURDAY, AUGUST 30th, 1890,

AT 3 O'CLOCK, P. M.

Or on Monday, Sept. 1st, in case of rain on Aug. 30th.

FIRST EVENT—DRESSING RACE. (GYMKHANA.)

Conditions. Ponies to be brought to the starting point with only a bridle on. Saddle, coat and waistcoat of rider to be on the ground. After the starting signal is given, each competitor (without any outside assistance) to saddle, girth his pony, put on his waistcoat and coat, and make the best of his way to the winning post, where he is to arrive with his waistcoat and coat entirely buttoned. Waistcoats to have at least five buttons, coats at least three buttons.—First and second prizes.

SUBSCRIBERS.	COLORS.	SUBSCRIBERS.	COLORS.
1. James W. Gerard, Jr.,	Pink.	7. Philip T. Penrose,	White.
2. Ellerton L. Dorr, Jr.,	Brown.	8. C. G. Lafarge,	Red.
3. Henry Phelps Case,	Dark Blue.	9. Moncure Robinson, 3d,	
4. Robt. L. Morrell,	Violet.		Light blue.
5. Gordon Prince,	Green.	10. A. C. Humbert,	Silver.
6. John B. Morris,	Yellow.		

SECOND EVENT—SACK RACE. BY INDIANS.

THIRD EVENT—MANIKIN RACE. (GYMKHANA.)

Conditions. Each competitor to ride to a point where manikins will be placed, and to carry one to the winning post on his pony.—First and second prizes.

SUBSCRIBERS.	COLORS.	SUBSCRIBERS.	COLORS.
1. A. C. Humbert,	Silver.	7. John B. Morris,	Yellow.
2. C. G. Lafarge,	Red.	8. Philip T. Penrose,	White.
3. Henry Phelps Case,	Dark blue.	9. Moncure Robinson, 3d,	
4. Ellerton L. Dorr, Jr.,	Brown.		Light blue.
5. Robt. L. Morrell,	Violet.	10. Gordon Prince,	Green.
6. James W. Gerard, Jr.,	Pink.		

FOURTH EVENT—POTATO & BUCKET RACE. GYMKHANA.

Conditions. Each competitor to place three potatoes in separate buckets distributed between starting and winning points. First in, after placing all three potatoes in their respective buckets, wins.—First and second prizes.

SUBSCRIBERS.	COLORS.	SUBSCRIBERS.	COLORS.
1. Robt. L. Morrell,	Violet.	6. Gordon Prince,	Green.
2. John B. Morris,	Yellow.	7. A. C. Humbert,	Silver.
3. Henry Phelps Case,	Dark blue.	8. C. G. Lafarge,	Red.
4. James W. Gerard, Jr.,	Pink.	9. Philip Penrose,	White.
5. Moncure Robinson, 3d,		10. Ellerton L. Dorr, Jr.,	Brown.
	Light blue.		

FIFTH EVENT—POTATO RACE.

SIXTH EVENT—CIGAR & UMBRELLA RACE. GYMKHANA.

Conditions. Ponies to be brought to the starting point with saddle and bridle, rider to be on the ground to receive cigar, matches and umbrella, after starting signal is given, each competitor, without any outside assistance, to light cigar, put up umbrella, mount and make the best of his way to the winning post, where he is to arrive with cigar lighted, umbrella open and in good order, (umbrella must remain open during the entire race.) —First and second prizes.

SUBSCRIBERS.	COLORS.	SUBSCRIBERS.	COLORS.
1. John B. Morris,	Yellow.	7. Philip T. Penrose,	White.
2. A. C. Humbert,	Silver.	8. Gordon Prince,	Green.
3. James W. Gerard, Jr.,	Pink.	9. Ellerton L. Dorr, Jr.,	Brown.
4. Henry Phelps Case,	Dark blue.	10. Moncure Robinson, 3d,	
5. C. G. Lafarge,	Red.		Light blue.
6. Robert L. Morrell,	Violet.		

SEVENH EVENT—BICYCLE CONTEST.

with cigars and umbrellas, conditions the same as in the 6th event. First and second prizes.

EIGHTH EVENT—EGG AND SPOON RACE. GYMKHANA.

Conditions. Each competitor to receive a wooden spoon with an egg in it to be carried with one hand to the winning post without breaking it. Should the egg fall, the competitor to replace it in the spoon, without assistance, and start again from the point where it fell, or he may return to the starting post for another egg. First and second prizes.

SUBSCRIBERS.	COLORS.	SUBSCRIBERS.	COLORS.
1. Gordon Prince,	Green.	7. Moncure Robinson, 3d,	
2. John B. Morris,	Yellow.		Light blue.
3. Henry Phelps Case,	Dark blue.	8. A. C. Humbert,	Silver.
4. James W. Gerard, Jr.,	Pink.	9. C. G. Lafarge,	Red.
5. Ellerton L. Dorr, Jr.,	Brown.	10. Robert L. Morrell,	Violet.
6. Philip T. Penrose,	White.		

FURTHER CONDITIONS FOR THE GYMKHANA RACES.

Open to horses of all ages and sizes. Catch weights.

Entrance free. The decisions of the Race Committee, or of such persons as it may appoint to be judges or starters, shall be final.

Following the Gymkhana there occurred an almost macabre incident at Kebo. At about three o'clock A.M. someone reported to the Bar Harbor police that a man was hanging from the rafters in the club's living room. The constabulary found an unprotesting gentleman jockey, participant in the events of the previous gala afternoon, swinging quietly from a rope, not around his neck, but trussed under the arms. Cut down, the unharmed reveler had no memory as to how he had reached his exalted state. Facts pieced together later, however, revealed that his position was attained at the hands of some of his fellow horsemen, celebrating the end of a glittering Kebo season.

By 1896 it was an opulent Bar Harbor. Mansions were everywhere. As one

Stanwood, home of James C. Blaine.

drove in toward town from the mainland, large "cottages" were dotting the shores of Hull's Cove, Frenchman Bay and the Shore Path, thinning out only as they approached Sand Beach. Also on the hills above the village, and toward Kebo, along the Eagle Lake Road, summer palaces were coming into being. An 1895 issue of the Bar Harbor *Record* said without restraint:

"Thus it will be seen that the word 'Cottages' does not convey the correct idea of the homes of Bar Harbor summer colonists. There are hundreds of thousands of dollars spent yearly in additions and alterations and the trend seems to be to build more costly places each year. A few years ago, before Bar Harbor's fame as a summer resort was world-wide, those who dwelt here in the summer were content with a simple home, but since fashion and wealth have adopted her for their own, they try to outbid each other. Most of the residences are in the midst of beautifully terraced lawns or are approached through large tracts of forest. The skill of the landscape artist is visible everywhere and they transform the primeval forests and rough land into attractive rural retreats and rolling lawns. Their broad smooth lawns sloped down to the bay. . . . In the background are the forest and mountains; in front are the bay and the mountains of the distance mainland." *Baymeath,* built in 1896 by J. T. Bowen of Chicago was situated far along the shore at Hull's Lane. "It was a great white house of attractive colonial style; from its broad esplanade on the bay side, would be obtained the most sweeping view of Bar Harbor and Frenchmans Bay."
In the distance rises *The Turrets,* the home of Mrs. J. J. Emery which is built of granite, after the plan of an old French castle *Stanwood,* where in summer lived Maine's noted statesman, James G. Blaine [who almost became President of the United States], stood nearby. "At *Stanwood* gathered the leading men of the country in politics and finance."

The Bar Harbor *Record* delved into its box of superlatives to describe Kenarden Lodge, the home of John Stewart Kennedy, railroad king in the days of Jesup, Hill and Harriman. Later Kenarden was owned by Mrs. John T. Dorrance of Philadelphia and after her death was torn down in 1960.

> "It cost over $200,000," said the *Record*, "and had its own electric power plant and at night when its hundred of incandescents are lit, it looks like a fairy palace to one gliding in a canoe or yacht over the cool waters of Frenchmans Bay. Then there is *Chatwold,* that quaint pile of architecture along the coast of Bear Brook. Here Joseph Pulitzer of the New York World spends the summer with his family. Last year, over $100,000 was expended upon it and this year $40,000 more is being laid out to suit the fastidious tastes of the owner. This year [1896], James A. Garland of New York will build the *Willows* on Eden Street, estimated to cost $150,000 and Edgar Scott of Philadelphia will spend a like sum on a summer home at Cromwell's Harbor, near the homes of George Vanderbilt and J. S. Kennedy."

The town became in truth a social capital of the United States so that the writer of a guidebook in 1890 could say of those walking down Main Street: "Here comes Peepy Marshmallow and Lina Van Rooster, Chicky Chalmers and Poodle Van Ulster, and the Hon. Hare Hare; and there in the background in the moire and black lace, are Mrs. Gatling Gun and Mrs. Wellman Heisdeick, and even Mrs. Stylington Ribblehurst herself."

Rank and fashion had come to the village and had changed its ways. Some might not like it. A flower painter, a Miss Ellen Robbins, would say, as she moved away, "If I were to come again next year, I should expect to see the trees all decorated with lace flowers and bows of ribbons."

The first decade of Kebo was indicative of the nineties — with teas, calls, horses, and parties and, since 1892, that fascinating new game, golf, to sweeten life. With no income tax, a plethora of servants, and eggs twenty cents a dozen, joy could be unrestrained.

Steamers were approaching Mount Desert from every sea lane. In fact, until 1934 Mount Desert was served by several steamship lines, which made travel from Boston, Portland, and other parts pleasanter and far more picturesque than the trains and motorcars which displaced them. In those more leisurely days it was possible to journey between almost all East Coast communities by water, but the Old Fall River Line and the Night Boat to Albany long have been left to the dubious mercy of raconteurs.

The steamer *Olivette* represented one of the strangest transportation lines ever to serve Mount Desert. She was owned by the operator of a southern line. When he was unable to persuade the head of a railroad system to furnish him with a special car, the outraged steamship magnate retorted: "I'll fix your road," and sent for the *Olivette.* For two years she plied between Boston and the island in competition with the railroad and travelers between the two points were furnished with the pleasantest form of transportation they ever enjoyed. The big *J. T. Morse* was one of the best known steamers that served the island. She picked

Bar Harbor boat landing.

up her passengers from the train at Rockland and brought them comfortably to Mount Desert.

At the turn of the century it cost little to travel to the remote island. Quoting a guide book, "Wagner cars . . . will be run from Chicago to Niagara Falls . . . through the White Mountains to Portland, where a change can be made to Bar

The steamboat wharf in Bar Harbor, about 1900.

Chatwood, home of newspaper mogul Joseph Pulitzer.

Harbor cars. . . . Wagner drawing rooms from Chicago, per chair, $5.50. Boston to Philadelphia a sleeper per berth, $2.00. . . . The Boston Steamers are large, seagoing, side wheel vessels with spacious saloons. . . . Staterooms $1.50 and $2.00. . . The passenger steps on board the elegant steamer 'Sappho' and is ferried across the lovely waters of Frenchman's Bay."

Construction costs were inviting, as the same guidebook discloses: "Bar Harbor can boast of more beautiful and costly residences than any other watering-place in America. These residences are called 'cottages' and the term is apt to mislead a stranger. He will be totally unprepared for the handsome stately piles of architecture. Certainly 'love in a cottage' of such description would be a very pleasant state of affairs."

An eye-witness picture of the glittering past, was provided by the late Amory Thorndike, a Bostonian, who, in past years, lived in Maine and served in the legislature. He was burned out in the Bar Harbor fire, but rebuilt and lived in Bar Harbor the year around. A boy in pre-World War I days, his vivid memories of the fabulous colony were fortified by recollections of his father, Dr. Augustus Thorndike, and grandfather, Dr. Robert Amory.

"Practically everybody arrived on the island by boat," said Mr. Thorndike. "In those days it was thrilling to catch the first glimpse of mountains and the sea and to sniff the piney, salty air after a long and stuffy jorney on the parlor cars. For the

62

summer people, too, it was a daily feature to watch the boat come in, see who was on it, and meet your friends on the wharf. The elegant private carriages, the cut-unders and buckboards from 'livery-stables' lined up all over the wharf and the tumult and melee reached a peak when the steamer blew its whistle for a landing.

"At that time everything depended on servants. The average 'summer estate' would have at least ten, seven in the 'cottage', because you couldn't possibly get along without a second in the kitchen to cook for the servants themselves; a second waitress or butler and a second chambermaid; and at least three outside: a gardener, a coachman and a second man. The 'cottages' therefore, had to have seven servants' rooms (which accounts for their being so large), and you had to have a stable on the grounds, either with a tenement in it for the gardener's family or a separate house for him. You had a garden, of course, and a large lawn, and an 'avenue' or driveway of crunching gravel that required raking by the second man at least twice a week.

"There were ninety or more houses of this size or larger and about fifty such structures still stood after the fire. In addition to a stable full of horses and carriages, many of the summer people had their own yachts and private piers along the shore. When the Atlantic Squadron was in, or the New York or Eastern Yacht clubs, supplementing ferryboats, the summer resident's yachts and many other small craft, the harbor was a colorful and busy place indeed. And when the fog came in, it brought a fascinating symphony of boat whistles and bells as they groped their way in and out from the wharves.

"As Bar Harbor developed as a summer colony, it soon became apparent that many arrivals were lured there not by the splendor of the scenery and the island's

On this island's coast, noted for its chilly sea, landlocked Somes Sound's 70 degree summer water (when wind is right) lures swimming enthusiasts.

Sir Lobster is as vital to Maine's economy as lumber, the Aroostook potato, or the tourist. In 1951 Maine lobstermen caught 20 million pounds of the tasty crustaceans, 75% of the nation's total.

unexcelled climate, but through a human frailty — a real or imagined desire to be with the 'right' people or in 'society.'

Inevitably real estate values hit the ionosphere, greatly to the pleasure of two principal promotors, Charles How and De Grasse Fox. As 'Society' established itself in 'cottages,' the old hotels disappeared and new ones, more chic and more exclusive, took their place. It's doubtful if all the new hotels together could take care of as many guests (700-1,000) as the old Rodick House alone, but the new guest-lists made up in quality for what they lacked in quantity.

"As all these fabulous and rich people took over, the type of vacation activity changed too. The canoe club gave way to the swimming pool and tennis courts; the favorite nature-study walks and explorations were abandoned in favor of parties, tournaments and a horse show. A terrific number of luncheons, teas, dinners, dances, musicales, yachting excursions and picnics-with-butler service, kept everyone's engagement calendars filled for weeks ahead. The men sat around their club, the Reading Room, sipping highballs and talking stock market, playing cards for high stakes and swapping stories and gossip.* The women spent mornings doing the 'housekeeping' — not, of course, the housework — simply giving orders and inspecting the work of numerous servants. The children often, with governesses or tutors, swam in the pool, played tennis, strolled over mountain trails or went sailing. The intricacies of the wardrobe and the art of dressing kept many of the women closeted with their ladies maids for hours. Just to drive from one house for lunch to another house for tea in a carriage was time-consuming. Also 'calling' was an important function in the afternoons, leaving a

---

*But it should be mentioned that not all was frivolity and merriment. Barrett Wendell, the Harvard professor, writing in the Boston *Transcript* of 1896, said Bar Harbor had the best conversation in America.

Here nature has not been outraged by a modern highway. The Ocean Drive, at Otter Cliffs. Seaward is Great Head.

visiting card if the callee was not 'at home.' One had a pleasant drive, exercised the horses, and (what's more important) got credit for the call, even if the caller did not 'get in.'

"And so it went each year for thirty brilliant years, from the middle of June, mounting in a hectic crescendo 'til the middle of September. These were the golden days of the fabulous summer colony at Bar Harbor. They were ended rather abruptly, with World War I, by the servant problem and the income tax."

Thorndike referred to the capitalists of the Reading Room. The Reading Room and its predecessor, the Oasis, the first Bar Harbor social club, began offering seclusion and conviviality in 1874.

In 1887 the Reading Room was moved from its brown cottage to an oval shaped building designed by the Boston architect, William R. Emerson. This club was to last forty years, the reason for its demise given as financial. Today the original building continues in an extended design as the Bar Harbor Motor Inn. In its 90 year history it has served as a Yacht Club, equipped with a double-decker pier, been owned by the Maine Central Railroad; operated as the Shore Club, and in World War II as a U.S. Naval Base.

The Oasis Reading Room club held one unforgettable soiree. In 1887 the *Herald* noted that "An extra number of police were on duty to keep the big crowd of interested spectators from running over fully the newly graded lawn." The account makes clear that all the beauty and fashion of the Bar Harbor summer colony were in complete representation at the ball.

The Oasis Club was not to enjoy its name for long — only, in fact in "spirits," shall we say, for it was merged into a real oasis of sorts with the building in 1887 of

Mt. Desert Reading Room Pier (right) and the steamboat wharf used by the *Mt. Desert* and, later, the *J.T. Morse*, (left). The dark yacht in the background is J.P. Morgan's *Corsair*.

the Reading Room Clubhouse whose main function was to supply surreptitious liquors to its 307 members. The membership flourished, doubly content in the fact that its clubhouse supplied, not only a safe haven for imbibing, but also undisturbed refuge from the female. The formula worked exceedingly well for a time and a record of 405 members was reached in 1888. But the increasing growth of equally accessible drinking spots in a legally dry town began attracting the male animal. The Reading Room list dwindled to but 257 members by 1890.

A noteworthy event occurred at the Reading Room during a visit by the

Reception Day at the Bar Harbor Reading Room.

English Fleet at the time of the Boer War. A summer cottage tenant, demonstrating the prevailing anti-British sentiments of the day, introduced a discordant note by raising a Boer flag on a flagpole bought for the purpose. Horror-stricken police cut the halyards, the prankster was expelled from the "gentlemen's club," and the incident naturally became a front page story in the press.

In the old days a steel latticework pier extended from the site. Here yachts could land passengers; on the upper level tea was served.

J. P. Morgan's series of black *Corsairs* (the fourth measured 406 feet overall) often lay in the harbor or just outside. Harbor pollak was a breakfast must with Morgan when he visited the island. This intelligence alerted one of the waterside folk who did not acquaint Morgan of the fact that schools of this little fish could be seen swimming off the town pier or around the sides of his yacht. Instead he kept the banker supplied with the "rarity" at one dollar per pollack.

Sproul's Restaurant, which served the high bloods with the best of everything long before the advent of many private clubs, was notable. Dawn usually revealed a number of coachmen and attendants waiting outside asleep in victorias and cut-unders. After the season closed, Sproul sent bills to his patrons. One recipient of good memory protested mildly that he had maintained a clear head on his last visit and that he had paid his bill. "Think nothing of it," said Sproul. "We send out a lot of bills anyway. You'd be surprised how many pay them."

Bar Harbor was slightly bored by the Hope diamond. Its owner, Evalyn Walsh McLean, lived in a house on the Shore Path which contained a dining room frescoed with heads of her husband Ned and President Harding and other Washingtonians of the era.

In a day when we enjoyed pleasant relations with Moscow, the Russian ambassador planned a three-day visit to Bar Harbor; Ned McLean, eager to be his host, paid $1500 for the use of an unoccupied house next door. The deal was closed twenty-four hours before the ambassador's arrival. Fifty people were hired to cut the long grass, clear away the cobwebs and otherwise ready the weary mansion, including purchasing and sewing new curtains and procuring other necessary furnishings. The seventy-two-hour embassy was available on time, however.

Prior to the deal, McLean, when informed by A. Stroud Rodick, his Bar Harbor agent, that the owner wanted much too much money said, "She can't make me take it, can she? Then I guess I'll take it."

Some years afterwards the owners of the stark house, an old Boston family impervious to the pretensions of Bar Harbor new money folk, and considerably fonder of their New Brunswick farm, refused to cut the grass on their few acres of shore front. Mr. Ketterlinus of printing fame paid a nuisance price of $30,000 to be rid of the shrewd puritans.

Bar Harbor, which was officially Eden until 1918, gets its name from the bar extending to Bar Island. In early days, the Rodicks had raised sheep on the island and spun the wool into crude sailcloth for their vessels. Also, they maintained a fish weir off the west side of the island; more than once a whale was caught in its meshes. Bar Island, often called Rodick's Island,* is firmly attached to Bar Harbor and may be reached dry shod at low tide, was a place of importance. Here was the celebrated Canoe Club where the Penobscot Indians gave canoeing lessons. Marion Crawford wrote two volumes about the Bar Harbor of buckboards and flirtations. One entitled *Maidens Call it Love in Idleness* ends with the lady accepting the gentleman in a canoe. From a chaperonage point of view, canoeing was considered a safe activity, since an overzealous swain could easily be controlled in such an unstable craft.

Those who feared to bathe in the icy and often turbulent waters of the bay, and who mistrusted sailing craft confidently embarked in canoes. It was a profitable business for boatmen rescuing those who had forgotten the tides and had left their craft to float away while they explored the eighty-acre island.

Bar Island is famous for one of the most fantastic of fetes champetres, given by the Turkish Ambassador in honor of a wasp-waisted Philadelphian beauty, also summering at Bar Harbor. The full moon rode the northern skies in amazingly balmy air, lanterns swung from every tree and violins played behind bushes and mossy boulders.

The most lyric pen of Bar Harbor's late 19th century was wielded by William Sherman, who published a series of guidebooks. They are collector's items now, but they may be seen at the Bar Harbor Historical Society. The little volumes are full of amusing pen and ink drawings in which ladies and their escorts resemble Charles Dana Gibson characters. Bar Harbor's famous public relations expert beckoned the tourist with such passages as:

"There are the lakes, their virgin purity smiling as sweetly in the sunlight as though they had never known the icy fetters of winter. He can launch his boat, pulling in under the shadow of the mountain peaks, let go the anchor and give himself up to meditation. He can dream away the day in idle fancies, the silence unbroken save by the drum of the partridge calling to his mate, or the lazy splash of trout in pursuit of the heedless fly.

"The buckboard. . . . The gentle swaying motion of the board while travelling at full speed over the hilly roads is simply delightful. . . .

"A gentleman can take his lady canoeing along the shore, they can land and indulge in that time honored pastime of rocking, i.e., lounging among the rocks, with an umbrella or sunshade set to keep off inquisitive eyes and reading aloud or flirting as they may elect.

"The Porcupines, four rocky, wooded islands, stretching in a chain across the bay from Bar Island . . . on some of them are pretty grottos . . . on Long Porcupine is a large cavern only accessible at low water, where a boating party nearly came to grief . . . a lady and a gentleman being forced to stay over night in its dark recesses.

"The Rodick House, the largest hotel in the State of Maine . . . the ballroom called the 'fish pond.' Soon the young ladies found this a favorite place, and many a golden fish was caught by the fair anglers."

*Today, in part Acadia National Park, and in part Gouldsboro, a town seven miles across Frenchman Bay.

Looking up Northeast Harbor toward Asticou. Noting mackerel fishermen always anchored in this arm of the sea for refuge. Squire Kimball in the 1860's here set up a little store, first S. S. Pierce agency in New England.

———————

Although the bridge at the Trenton Narrows was erected as early as 1836 with fitting ceremony, including poetry, automobiles were not allowed on the island until 1915, and bitter was the battle before island voters relented.

As early as 1896, Paul Hunt, architect, had assembled an automobile at a time when some intrepid individuals were putting engines into buggies, first removing the shafts. Hale writes that in 1907 Leslie Brewer "built a car locally with a motorboat engine, but with a differential. . . . This moved legally about the unrestricted streets with some difficulty in steering, until the law was changed again."

Influential Mt. Desert Island summer residents, including S. Weir Mitchell, L. E. Opdycke, D. B. Ogden, and Joseph Pulitzer, worshippers of King Horse, and indulgent toward the joys of driving peacefully in a carriage, procured legislation which banned automobiles on the island. President Eliot of Harvard, one of the earliest of the early Northeast Harbor summer residents, led the fight against the smoking intruders. Likewise Arthur Train, revered creator of Mr. Tutt, wrote a skit describing the mayhem that would ensue on the day that saw the streets of Bar Harbor admitting cars.

The Great Automobile War continued. Unlike the rest of Maine, which had cars, a selected poll of Bar Harbor summer residents found them more than ninety per cent against (527 to 27). Among those outspoken in their favor was George W. Vanderbilt who, because of the action of the town, leased his cottage and went to Newport.

Eventually, permissive legislation allowed the towns of Mt. Desert Island to vote for or against automobiles and Eden voted for them, as Southwest Harbor had done some years before. Northeast Harbor, being of a more stubborn nature, was reluctant to allow the integration of the gas carriages, only to vote "yes" when a death occurred because a doctor had been obliged to drive by buggy from the town line.

———————

Bar Harbor's first intimate contact with World War I came with the unexpected arrival of the German ship, *Kronprinzessin Cecilie.*

On August 4, 1914, Bar Harbor awoke to find the huge North German Lloyd liner figuratively sitting on the front lawn. Her name had been painted out and she wore counterfeit markings on her four stacks. She had been days at sea, homeward bound with 1,216 passengers and $13,000,000 in gold bullion and bars when World War I reached explosive heat and she was told to avoid allied shipping and seek a secure haven.

The Kronprinzessin Cecilie at Bar Harbor, August 4, 1914.

Her skipper, Captain Charles Pollak, mindful that British warships might be watching larger ports, decided upon Bar Harbor. Probably he was influenced by one of his passengers, New York broker and Mount Desert yachtsman C. Ledyard Blair, who later piloted the big ship up Frenchman Bay.

For the Hinkle sisters, also *Cecilie* tourists from Mt. Desert, the leviathan's dawn arrival was like a strange dream. They wept fluently when confronted, not by the expected shores of Europe, but by the outline of their own Bar Harbor house.

The passengers departed by train and the treasure was carried ashore by the revenue cutter *Androscoggin*. Later the *Cecilie* steamed to Boston under a gentleman's agreement that she could go beyond the three-mile limit of territorial waters if necessary. Eventually, after this country entered the global conflict, the *Cecilie* became the transport *Mount Vernon* and carried many troops to fight against her homeland.

Bar Harbor's Haskell Hadley Cleaves, then twelve years old, recalls being awakened by his father in time to see from the Shore Path the *Cecilie* depart the harbor at 4 A.M. on a cold November day in 1914. She was escorted by a cutter and two destroyers; the early departure was occasioned to utilize as long as possible a daylight passage for the trip to Boston; there existed the fear of German submarines in an era long before radar and sonic devices.

Nor will Cleaves forget the unheralded arrival of the great ship the previous August. His senses remember acutely the horrendous blast of its great whistle, shaking a sleeping and puzzled Bar Harbor, breaking, as it were, the sound barrier of that day, rattling windows and echoing in the mountains.

When our informant was ten an incident occurred worth recounting: Cleaves remembers when Mrs. John R. McLean (mother-in-law of Evalyn Walsh McLean of Hope diamond fame, also a summer resident) lay ill in the structure on Cottage Street which is now the Central House. To protect the sensitivities of the patient, a thick carpet of wood shavings was laid down on the streets approaching the house from three sides, about one hundred yards each way. Thus were silenced the clopping of the hoofs of the horses pulling the buckboards and cut-unders and other equipages of the times. To attend the elderly Mrs. McLean, in this last illness, a celebrated physician was rushed from North Carolina, the sole occupant of a private train especially chartered for the purpose.

In 1925 the Edward Stotesburys arrived on the Bar Harbor scene and bought what most people considered a fine house on Frenchman Bay which had been owned by the family of A. J. Cassatt, President of the Pennsylvania Railroad. But it was not fine enough for Mrs. Stotesbury who tore it apart and started over, remodeling it not once, but twice; the first refurbishing cost $450,000, the second $650,000.

Clarence Dow, a former nurseryman, was reported in a Sunday newspaper feature that he did his first landscaping job on the grounds for $100,000. Later Dow was retained on an annual contract to take care of Mrs. Stotesbury's plants, which he says, "she wanted shifted every two weeks."

Dow moved 100 big pine trees, two feet thick and twenty five to thirty feet high from one location to another. He was also commissioned to scour the Bar Harbor area for ten full grown elm trees. They were moved and set up on the property at a cost of about $1,500 an elm.

Bar Harbor's Everett Lymburner, who did the electrical work, recalled several conferences with Mr. and Mrs. Stotesbury, her contractors and architects. Once when Mrs. Stotesbury wanted literally to raise the roof of Wingwood, as she called the millon dollar house, Mr. Stotesbury, whose nickname was "Little Sunshine," as always patiently inquired the cost. Then hopelessly, he substituted a benign smile in place of further pleas for economy. On this occasion he then ventured an aside to Lymburner, "I would prefer a small place and beans every Saturday night."

What emerged from the extensive remodeling was an eighty room house, a colonnaded main structure and two wings. Thirty-eight of the rooms were in the servants' wing. The house was heated by fifty-six electric wall heaters and five hot air furnaces which burned more than eighty tons of coal just to keep the temperature above freezing in winter. Heat was also provided by twenty-six hand-carved marble fireplaces imported from Europe. They were equipped with peculiar looking special electric heaters that resembled coal grates. These and other electrical fixtures were implemented by a 2,200 volt system controlled from

Wingwood, home of Mr. and Mrs. E. T. Stotesbury.

a large switch panel in an electrical vault which looked like a regulation power station. There were twenty-eight complete bathrooms; Mrs. Stotesbury's had a fabulous gold bathtub plus gold fittings. Queried once on the gold fixtures Mrs. Stotesbury gave a characteristic answer, "They're very economical," she said, "you don't have to polish them."

There were fifty-two telephone lines into the house and twenty-three extensions on the house system. Protection for the grandiose layout was provided

Canadian National M.V. *Bluenose* plies her constant twenty knots between Bar Harbor and Yarmouth, Nova Scotia; on board the road-weary gaze at the Bay of Fundy or indulge in hours of saturated sleep in deck chair or stateroom.

Bar Harbor — Yarmouth, Nova Scotia Ferry, completing its six-hour trip across Bay of Fundy.

by a burglar alarm which when activated set off a siren on each side of the house and a light went on in every room. A secret panel, high above the ballroom, gave a delightful arcane touch to the fabulous property.

Mr. Stotesbury died in 1938; Mrs. Stotesbury in 1946. Previous to her end the renowned spending had ceased. Whatever the hidden assets the visible Stotesbury cash flow, as far as the lay public was concerned, seemed to have slowed to a trickle.

> Cleveland Amory writes ". . . shortly before her death Mrs. Stotesbury wrote a friend who was at the moment visiting the author Booth Tarkington in Kennebunkport, Maine. Mrs. Stotesbury spoke feelingly of the difficulties of the new times, and then concluded with a postscript. 'Tell dear Mr. Tarkington,' she wrote, 'that I am reading all his old books. I can't afford to buy any new ones'."

Today the site is occupied by the Bar Harbor-Yarmouth Ferry Terminal.

The Bar Harbor Fire

THE great fire of 1947 was a crucible in which Mount Desert Island showed the world that her people were of the stuff of tensile steel.

Those who beat out the flames remember it as three weeks in which they seldom removed rubber boots from drawn and blistered feet. Benzedrine pills by the pocketfull kept them going without sleep for as long as five consecutive nights.

October, traditionally, is Mount Desert's most glorious month and 1947 was no exception. Indian summer held the island in a sultry and wanton embrace; occasionally the mercury touched eighty degrees.

There had been no rain since May. Tinder dry conditions extended throughout the state, the worst, according to the Maine Weather Bureau, in three hundred years. On the island earlier forest fires had been dispatched that summer by time-tested country methods and undoubtedly the great Bar Harbor Fire would have been disposed of in like manner had it not been for the three hours of almost hurricane wind in the late afternoon of Thursday, October 23.

Then Bar Harbor stole the front pages all over the world.

No one knows for certainty how it started, but the community had tolerated a supposedly harmless criminal in Dolliver's Dump all summer. Here a fire smoldered sullenly, occasionally bursting into sufficient flame to call for a nightly dousing but never complete extinction. The light winds that come up with dawn always found sufficient embers to fan into dangerous flame.

How did the fire actually start if not in Dolliver's Dump? It has been suggested that sun pouring through the glass of a discarded automobile or a bottle

The fire imposed a classic and dignified beauty: left, top, William P. Hamilton estate: right, Charles B. Pike ruins: lower left, Turkish Prince Burnahedin's garden. The fire burned spasmodically for days after the big blow.

acting as a magnifying glass could have been responsible. It is known only that the holocaust was born in the uninspiring vicinity of the dump where peat bogs can carry flame underground, and that no one appreciated the greatest threat Mount Desert ever faced until it was too late. The big wind of the twenty-third, a predicted but unbelievable gale, blew the flames past all opposition, and in less than three hours traveled six miles down a three-mile-wide track, took the piper's fee for man's mistake in underestimating the dire potentialities of a forest fire.

Spasmodic flames parried opposition for a week in the midland areas before establishing an upperhand on Tuesday, the twenty-first, the day the Army Air Corps fire fighters arrived from Dow Field, Bangor. The local authorities were asked to make decisions of strategy, for the fire was now "zigging" to Eagle Lake Road and McFarland's Hill and casting toward Sargent Mountain and Northeast Harbor, in fact a two-pronged fire that had crossed the Norway Drive and penetrated the Sunken Heath (Mount Desert pronunciation: "haith"), entered the out-of-control stage. Embers and clots of flame rode on the wind from treetop to treetop, seeming to carry the fire ahead of itself in a destructive game of leap-frog. Dried branches and slash hissed and flared like last week's Christmas tree.

The loneliness of evacuation . . . Talleyrand corner.

The hot foot. This little tyke danced through the holocast and survived. The statue was all that John D. Archbold salvaged when the great fire destroyed his Mount Desert summer home. These ruins also contained a dumbwaiter that obediently appeared on well-ordered missions in the center of the dining room table at its mistress' bidding.

Tree trunks, though green in appearance, under the pressure of interior moisture suddenly expanded by the intense heat, exploded like musketry; in the forests there were sounds as if wooden walls were being torn by a giant ripper. Fire fighters said there were two fires: one aloft (the crown fire) in the treetops and the other on the forest floor traveling on an incendiary carpet of dried autumn leaves, fir and pine needles.

As the fury increased assistance came from off island — Camden, Bucksport, Belfast, Blue Hill, Ellsworth, Orono, Old Town, and Dow Field, Bangor. National Park authorities flew in experts in forest fire control from distant Florida and the Great Smokies. And the Navy, and Coast Guard, steaming from Boston through heavy seas arrived at 7 a.m. Friday, October 24, with the Army earlier on the scene; all service branches proved their value without actually declaring martial law. Later it was learned that guardsmen were issued but one cartridge each.

By Wednesday the 22nd there was a positive acknowledgment that the town had a real fire on its hands. The Chief of Police requested that the State Liquor Store be closed for the duration of the emergency. This was done, the first move of

Schooner Head woods, vortex of the flame. (Right) Bell on Satterlee estate . . . but not the knell of Bar Harbor.

its kind since Maine went wet in 1933, and without waiting for an act of legislature.

After the evacuation on "Black Thursday" eventually women volunteers and the Red Cross worked night and day to provide food and creature comforts. Exhausted men caught brief naps on the floor of the Bar Harbor Fire House, the command center, between calls to duty on the ever-shifting fire lines. The well learned practice of Civilian Defense remembered from war days had workable application.

It was the type of fire in which predatory instincts of wild animals are suspended in common peril and the fox and wildcat, the rabbit and deer seek safety in close proximity in water-filled ditches or ponds. Such a parallel emerges from the Bar Harbor fire for on one critical night, there was a call for a pair of volunteers from a burning area deep in the woods, where there was a possibility of being trapped. Two men who long had been unspeaking enemies stepped forward, leaped aboard a small truck and sped away to the danger zone, but not to eternal flame.

As for the climax blow on the afternoon of October twenty-third: Just as sparks were flying across the shore road at Hull's Cove towards the coastal show places, the southwest wind stopped dead. There was an ominous respite and then a gale whistled out of the northwest. The fire quadrupled its speed in a new direction and took off toward Bar Harbor town but away from the shores of Frenchman Bay, leaping Breakneck Road, Witch Hole and Fawn Ponds like a blowtorch under forced draft. The cluster of pumping engines including Mt.

Snaking up Cadillac Mountain... three miles of hose. The late "Doc" Ells, perennial greeter of fleets, and accordingly holder of a Navy citation, with two fire-fighting sailors from a destroyer... the tars have been ocean swimming in weather exceptionally warm for late October.... Note sooty rocks.

Desert Township companies, Northeast and other island brigades working at Hull's Cove, were now cut off from access to Bar Harbor.

The full gale was now in command. The Coast Guard Cutter, *Laurel*, hurrying to the aid of Bar Harbor, recorded by instruments, while sixty miles away, a wind velocity of seventy knots.

Residents across Frenchman Bay are forever sounding off how Bar Harborites sit on their famous view. Now these off-islanders saw that shore line as they would never see it again, the billows of smoke and flame flying across the lower hills, like the sweep of clouds in a Guido Reni chromo. Fishermen of Lamoine, Hancock Point, Sullivan, Gouldsboro, Sorrento and Winter Harbor put out across the Bay expecting to assist in an American Dunkirk. As they approached the Bar Harbor pier it was necessary to pick holes in the smoke — they called it "navigating by the seat of their pants," a human equivalent of radar.

Meanwhile, following orders, four thousand Bar Harbor folk not actually engaged in fire fighting, with whatever property they could manage — one pair transported a refrigerator — removed to the athletic field. Through the slightly bewildered but joking crowd a woman methodically pursued her lost cat up and down the field by beating on a pan with a spoon; Tabby, accustomed to this method of reconnaissance, eventually appeared.

New reports of the approaching fire seemed to indicate that the field might lie in its path; word was passed to the patient gathering to remove to the town pier. Shadowy forms, like refugees of war, began the half-mile march in the

The Jackson Laboratory two days after the fire.

choking dusk, a darkness accentuated by smoke. Some left belongings on the field; others as they marched dropped suitcases and bundles behind hedges along Main Street — for safekeeping and to lighten the burden.

On reaching the wharf floodlights revealed the picture of giant waves making escape by sea frightening. With the night came bitter cold, the first frosty autumn evening in weeks. The wind was due north.

By 9:30 a command came over the loud-speaker for cars to make a dash for the mainland by shore highway 3. Bulldozers opened a path through the ruins of the De Gregoire Hotel and a long motorcade wetted by fire hoses for good measure, conveyed by state policemen and led by seven buses filled mostly with elderly people, ran the gauntlet of flame and flying ash, carrying the majority out of the danger zone and into the protection of Ellsworth.

Earlier that afternoon about 3:30 or 4:00, the evacuation signal 7-7 had sounded. All who could were advised to get off the island. The road by Sieur de Monts Spring and the Tarn, although full of smoke, was still unscorched; a company of foresighted individuals whose automobiles were not required for fire fighting started around the flank of the fire, some 700 cars taking in stragglers as they went via Otter Creek and Seal Harbor to the head of Somes Sound and to Town Hill — eventually to the safety of the mainland. This daylight motor file heading into a blinding haze of smoke and the setting sun, running bumper to bumper over a twenty-mile shore line course at never more than 25 miles per hour, was composed mostly of women drivers. No traffic accidents occurred.

Meanwhile, like an express train that has passed through the edge of town, the fire drove overland for the open sea, having leveled in its path several hotels

Flames plus vandals: W.P. Hamilton pool. (Right) one of the more artistic ruins.

as well as dwellings on the secondary hills, and the Highbrook Road, Eagle Lake Road, Kebo and Strawberry Hill areas. Later Champlain Mountain, Schooner Head and the Beehive were to be seared before the wind drove the main column of flame out over the ocean a mile beyond Great Head, an unsupported black cloud with a flaming core of burning resinous vapor.

This long arc of flame turned back little boats from the adjacent islands. They returned next day to Northeast Harbor, laden with homebaked pies, cakes and bread for the fire fighters' canteens.

The conflagration was still out of control and remained so at least until the twenty-fifth, and long after the fire, like a mortally wounded dragon, continued to blow its hot breath on whatever combustible it could reach, giving weary fire fighters little rest. The "all-out" signal was not sounded until November seventh, and weeks later, after snow had fallen, fire smoldered in peat four feet below the surface of Sieur de Monts Meadows.

The outbreak of numerous fires, near but unrelated to the major conflagration, had furnished a mystery, until it was learned they were set, but not by an intentional incendiary. Raccoon, notoriously curious creatures, too often lingered until fur ignited, then raced away and rolled in dry leaves or needles in frenzied efforts to smother the fire. An Acadia National Park naturalist, Wilbur Doudna, contributed one believe-it-or-not eyewitness incident: he saw a set of Siamese twin raccoons who were joined at the shoulder moving ahead of the fire and apparently making their escape.

Loss of wildlife was not heavy. Five burnt deer carcasses were reported by a survey of a group from the University of Maine, The Maine Co-operative Wild

Melted lead urn on Mrs. William S. Moore estate. (Right) The builder said, "the fireplace will outlast everything in your house," but a few hours after the fire citizens of Bar Harbor, fearful lest towers and chimneys might tumble, leveled every such relic.

Life Research Unit. Usually deer with their great speed can run through or outdistance flame; but this conflagration was too fast and covered too wide an area. A few partridges were unable to fly over the top of the crown fire.

Property damage was great. Five of Bar Harbor's hotels were destroyed; sixty-seven of the two hundred and twenty-two summer cottages and one hundred and seventy of six hundred and sixty-seven permanent homes. The Jackson Laboratory was gone and about 10,000 acres of Acadia National Park was consumed. A ball of flame alighted on the old brick Hamor house at Hulls Cove and it was almost instantly consumed.

At the height of the fire it became apparent that pay for volunteer fire fighters could bankrupt the town and announcement was made that there would be no recompense for such services. But this failed to slacken efforts of the volunteers, one hundred and seventy of whom had lost their own homes.

Despite the magnitude of the 23 million dollar disaster, loss of life was light. An elderly man, ignoring advice, entered his home a third time to save a cat and did not return. A girl was killed in a traffic accident, and a man and a woman, already ill, succumbed to heart attacks.

On Eagle Lake Road, one of the areas gutted most by the fire, a celebrated Siamese cat kennel, cats included, was a total loss.

There were close calls for humans: some of the Rockefeller foresters and a group of the University of Maine volunteers, who were holding the line of the

Open checkroom on the athletic field. But neither the rain came . . . nor the flame. (Right) The Jackson Laboratory asbestos mice . . . survivors but sterile.

Northeast Harbor side of Eagle Lake Road during Thursday's blast, found themselves trapped before oncoming sheets of flames. Diving into Aunt Betty's pond, they submerged for the better part of an hour, safe in the knowledge that their heads would be unscathed in a breathing space of a foot or two that always

A house that escaped the flames — possibly the oldest on the Island.

Fire relic, the Pike house.

Former site of Malvern Hotel at Tallyrand Corner now occupied by a modern motel.

Great Head, well seaward of Sand Beach, highest headland on the Atlantic Coast, the jumping-off place of the Fire. Riding in the wings of an almost hurricane wind, a great black cloud with a glowing orange core, rolled a mile or more out over the sea. It was here that fishermen from Northeast Harbor, the Cranberries and other islands were turned back by raging seas and the danger of igniting their sails and rigging.

exists between flame and the surface of water. Another spectacular incident occurred on a smoking woodsroad at night when a rampaging deer knocked a volunteer off the running board of a moving truck. The fire fighter's injuries were gory but not fatal.

The Paris *Figaro* on its front page screamed "La ville de Bar Harbor est a demi detruite." *Le Figaro* tried to imply that Bar Harbor had been fired by Maine peasants protesting great landed estates. Actually, the gardeners and caretakers saved many of the large houses in their charge by wetting down roofs until flames forced them off.

The fire swept over 17,000 acres of the island's forest cover. Literally, the

(Above) The Building of Arts before it was destroyed by the '47 Fire. It was the scene of concerts by such as Kreisler and Paderewski.

(Below) The Jackson Laboratory two years after the fire . . . rebuilt and larger.

situation looked black after the fire had passed, and hope for a quick regrowth of new vegetation was dim. But nature has done a marvelous job in reclothing the burned area. Today, evidence of the fire are the birches and aspens. The cone-bearing trees are gradually coming back.

PHOTO: COURTESY OF THE BAR HARBOR HISTORICAL SOCIETY, JESUP MEMORIAL LIBRARY, BAR HARBOR.

Acadia National Park — The Triumph of George B. Dorr

A grant far more durable and realistic than those bestowed upon Sieur de Monts and the others has been made of thousands of Mount Desert's most beautiful acres.

That area, more than two-fifths of the island, has been given in perpetuity to the federal government as part of the vast Acadia National Park, and as such is a wildlife sanctuary. It was the first national park east of the Mississippi and the first to be evolved entirely from privately owned land, thanks to the generosity of a small group who determined to preserve for posterity the original splendor of one of the most excitingly beautiful sections of the country.

John A. Peters, Congressman from Ellsworth, and uncommonly well acquainted with eastern Maine, said that "the portable sawmill created Acadia National Park." He meant it was the threat of this instrument of scenic mayhem that sparked a crusade which saved the island from ruthless spoilation by lumbermen.

Charles W. Eliot, President Emeritus of Harvard and original summer landowner at Northeast Harbor, incited to action by his landscape-architect son, C. W. Eliot, Jr., realized the portable mill brought hitherto inaccessible mountain timber within the reach of the buzz saw. Dr. Eliot knew erosion would quickly follow removal of the timber and soon the island literally would become a desert. To rescue and protect Mt. Desert for future generations to enjoy, Eliot, a keen judge of men, chose a rare individual — a wealthy Boston bachelor named George Bucknam Dorr.

On August 12, 1901, President Eliot wrote Dorr that he was convening a

Pointing the lens into the midmorning sun . . . lobster boat plus steadying sail off Schoodic Point, Acadia National Park. This granite headland juts further into the Atlantic than any other Maine promontory.

meeting at the Music Room on Rowland Road in Seal Harbor to confer with various members of the Village Improvement Societies of Seal, Northeast and Bar Harbors for the purpose of organizing a group of trustees to hold reservations at points of interest on the island, for the perpetual use of the public.

Dorr corraled John S. Kennedy, George Vanderbilt and William J. Schieffelin, his neighbors on the Bar Harbor shore. The group steamed around to Seal in Mr. Kennedy's yacht, which conveniently lay off his mammoth estate, Kenarden, bordering on Cromwell Harbor. The Right Reverend William Lawrence, Bishop of Massachusetts, drove over by carriage.

President Eliot presided at the meeting and stated its purpose. A vote to organize was passed; Dorr became executive officer. When Maine's biennial legislature next convened, on January 1, 1903, a charter was obtained recognizing the public-service character of the corporation and — most importantly — making it free of tax.

The official language of the charter stated that the purpose was "to acquire, by devise, gift, or purchase, and to own, arrange, hold, maintain, or improve for public use lands in Hancock County, Maine, which by reason of scenic beauty, historical interest, sanitary advantage or other like reasons may become available for such purpose."

Two gifts followed the incorporation. The first was a rod-square site on top of a bold cliff on the picturesque, ocean-fronting Cooksey Drive, later to be occupied by a commemorative tablet recording the visit of Champlain in 1604. The second gift was almost equally modest: a hilltop overlooking Jordan Pond, favorite walk with the summer visitors at Seal Harbor.

The cruel sea . . . morning after October storm, Thunder Hole, Bar Harbor.

For the following five years the corporation slept. No gifts were bestowed, no efforts made to acquire them, no toes stepped on.

In September of 1908, Dorr lay in bed at his Storm Beach House in Bar Harbor, recovering from a surgical operation which had necessitated his missing the annual September meeting of the Trustees. But late that afternoon President Eliot dropped in on the convalescent to report that they had just received their first important gift, the Bowl and Beehive tract on Newport (now Champlain) Mountain. The Bowl, a delightful little pond, lies four hundred feet above the sea, just north of the Beehive Headland, both overlooking the crescent Sand Beach and miles of open sea. This was a gift to excite Dorr's imagination, ideally suited to the Trustees' purpose, wild, beautiful and unique. Dorr told Eliot that as soon as he was on his feet again he would attempt to annex the summit of Green (now Cadillac) Mountain, the highest in a ring of island peaks, offering a dramatic view hardly excelled anywhere — a 360-degree sweep of ocean, lakes, islands and forest, an entire Down East panorama spreading out below, an enormous relief map.

As soon as Door was up and about he went straight to John S. Kennedy, a member trustee of the original Hancock County group. He at once agreed to help in acquiring the summit of the mountain. After receiving Kennedy's promise of financial assistance, Dorr let no grass grow under his feet. He took immediate steps to discover the owners of the summit tract. A succession of beautiful Indian summer days were spent on the mountain with his legal advisor, Harry Lynam, tracing out and identifying the bounds of the tract they sought.

The desired land, which lay within a single huge lot, had been obtained by Daniel Brewer, descendant of one of the early settler families of the town. His father, Edward Brewer of Hull's Cove, was known far and wide as "Master" Brewer because about the middle of the eighteenth century he built most of the vessels of Mt. Desert. With his profits from shipbuilding and logging, the "Master" purchased the top of the mountain, plus a broad extent of forest land below, from the Bingham heirs of Philadelphia. At that time the Bingham estate held vast stretches of eastern Maine which had been acquired at the end of the last century for their timber value.

The Cadillac Mountain transaction was consummated in jig time. The forceful combination of Dorr and Kennedy had gained a priceless possession for the Trustees and the as yet unborn Acadia.

Springs had from boyhood held a singular interest for George Dorr, an attraction heightened by his many trips to Europe, where "from earliest times they have been objects of mystery." The spring now known as Sieur de Monts, truly magnificent, with its constant flow of clean water, was sunk deep in the spruce near the Great Meadow's southern end, close by the old Indian trail which passed along the foot of Champlain Mountain on its way to the Gorge and thence to Otter Creek. Hidden by the concealing woods and with the mountains rising steeply behind, it was unknown even to Dorr until two townsfolk began to build a pump house and bottle the water commercially on land owned by the Rodick brothers, Serenus and Fountain. The Rodicks had let out an option to the developers, who in turn had found rough going financially. When work came to a halt, Dorr at once attempted to determine at what figure the spring lands could be obtained. The price was high: five thousand dollars. He went no further, entering only into an agreement with the lessor, one Ora Strout, not to sell to anyone else without first permitting him to buy. "And," Dorr says in his papers, "there the matter rested; there seemed no need for haste."

Then one spring day in 1909, when Dorr was out on the hills checking on the work in hand, Harry Lynam drove up breathlessly: "Mr. Lynam said to me [Dorr wrote]:

> "Mr. Dorr, a bunch of them up town have got together and raised the money to take over the option on the spring, which they believe to be essential to your plans. Ora Strout gives you until noon to take it, but will sell to them upon the stroke of twelve unless you close with him first. Cash in hand, they are waiting by the clock on the Village Green till noon shall come to make the purchase. What will you do?"
>
> This was in the old, slow horse-driving days. Mr. Lynam had spent some time in search of me and when he found me there was but a scant fifteen minutes left in which to reach the Village Green, a mile or more away. There was no time to spare. I made up my mind on the spot to take the option, and Mr. Lynam drove back as rapidly as the team which had brought him down could carry him, to so tell Mr. Strout. He found him waiting on the Village Green, where were also gathered the group that sought to take the option from me, waiting, cash in hand, for the hour to strike. When Mr. Lynam drove up, with but two or three minutes to spare, and told Mr. Strout that I would take it, they could not conceal their anger and hot words ensued between them and Strout. But the spring was mine, and became, as it proved, one of the foundation stones on which the future park was built.

The great granite block walling the Otter Creek Gorge fell next to the Dorr banner. This acquisition commenced the same year as the Cadillac triumph, 1908.

Cathedral aisle to Otter Cliffs, Acadia National Park.

Sea weed on Sand Beach, a rare occurrence, but here deposited following an Autumn "line storm."

The following fall Dorr presented the Trustees with one of several gifts over the years from his own property. This section, an inheritance from his father, was full of sentimental association for the donor:

> This was a tract where, following rains, Bear Brook comes tumbling down the ravine between Picket Mountain [Huguenot Head] and Champlain to enter a basin at the bottom called Beaver Dam Pool from the relics of old beaver dams which it contained and the presence of an occasional beaver still to be seen swimming in it. A reedy margin surrounded it and giant hemlocks and yellow birches grew round about.
>
> Around the pool and winding among the ancient forest trees, I had built, a dozen years before, for my friends' and the public's use, a broad bicycle path, at a time when a new development of geared machines and rubber-tubed tires had given a new popularity to the bicycle, and everyone who could was riding.
>
> The Bicycle Path, just wide enough for my mother to pass through in her little one-horse buckboard, became a favorite drive for her in days of mellow autumn sunshine, where she could quietly watch the yellow birch leaves change and fall. But now, my mother gone, I wanted to make a gift to the public, through the Reservations, of this land in which she had found such happiness.

George Dorr could scarcely talk of his mother without tears coming to his eyes. She was a Miss Mary Ward of Boston, a regal personality, good-looking and positive. Cleveland Amory in *The Last Resorts* speaks of her thus:

> One lady who showed a mind of her own and at the same time furthered the tradition of Bar Harbor's conversation was the mother of George B. Dorr, author of Bar Harbor's first formal garden, who prided herself on her ability to name every point of interest on Mt. Desert. Once, questioned at tea by an officious

visitor about some particularly remote spot, she was stumped, but only
momentarily. "We never answer questions here," she said, "after four o'clock."

In the last decade of Door's life he was without adequate sight, but during his
Harvard years he was suddenly stricken completely blind. His mother led him to
Europe and the great specialists. Without recourse to an operation, his seeing was
miraculously restored; he was able to resume his studies at Harvard, and later at
Oxford. Later, Dorr often spoke of his mother's intense interest in "psychical
research," possibly applied at the time.

Dorr inherited a fortune from both sides; at one time the family worth was
estimated in the vicinity of ten million dollars. He himself paid no attention to his
estate over the years, believing it sufficient to withstand his incessant purchasing
of Park lands. Early, however, had come the dwindling of the Dorrs' New
England textile holdings. Impervious to all such rumblings, with syndicate help
(and eventually the largesse of a Rockefeller) Dorr pursued the granite and the
spruce. In the beginning he spurned a salary as the first official Director of the
Sieur de Monts Monument; by the time of the creation of Acadia National Park,
he would gladly accept the department's salary — in fact, his only real cash at
retirement.

Beyond the Dorr ownership lay Huguenot Head, with its bold, southward-
facing cliff looking out across the sea. This dramatic area and some neighboring
portions of Champlain Mountain would round out Dorr's most recent gift.

> For this, writes Dorr, "I went to Mr. Kennedy who once more willingly
> agreed to aid. No papers passed between us; his word was enough. I promptly
> got in touch with the owners, who held the tract only for its lumber value, and
> made an agreement with them for the purchase of the land. While I was still at
> work with them, searching out its bounds, Mr. Kennedy left for his winter home
> in New York. Soon I heard that he was ill of pneumonia; then word came
> suddenly that he had died. It was a great loss to me and I felt it deeply. It left me,
> also, in a difficult situation as regards the land he had offered to buy, for I had
> entered into a definite agreement with the owners for its purchase.
> But it had happened, most movingly to me, that the last words his wife had
> heard him utter, as she bent over him to hear what he might say, were:
> "Remember . . . that I promised Mr. Dorr . . . to help him get that land."

The next tract he acquired, which turned out to be extremely important in
the development of what it led to — the granted power of eminent domain — had
to do with protecting the water supply of Eagle Lake. Chance brought the
opportunity; he did not seek it.

A prominent Bar Harbor summer resident, Philip Livingston Livingston,
had made plans to build a summer house under the guise of a camp, above an old
wood road which encircled the beautiful high ground on the western side of Eagle
Lake, the source of Bar Harbor's drinking water. Apparently there was no
opportunity to drain the building away from the lake, whose high-level waters
were esteemed for their purity.

Dorr reports that the sale was made quietly and work on the construction

Northeast Harbor softened by its traditional fog. Skippers from outer islands seek shelter here in dirty weather. In summer, this excellent anchorage greets Atlantic yachts. Protected by the Schoolhouse Ledges, the Asticou Terraces and the "Kimball Calm" . . . "home is the sailor" is a reality. This is the farthest "Down East" for most cruises, the final triumphant moment.

not begun until late fall, when most of the summer residents had reached their winter homes. Soon thereafter a Mt. Desert newspaper, whose loyal subscribers followed its news throughout the winter from metropolitan bases, sprang the fact of the Eagle Lake development in an enthusiastic report. The reaction from distant readers was not quite what the editor had expected.

The water company's directors, chosen from leading summer residents, promptly met in New York and decided that the construction of the projected building must be stopped at any cost. "I was not a member of that board," Dorr relates, "but all knew my interest in what concerned Bar Harbor; and their chairman, Mr. William Lee, was instructed to write me in Boston asking if I, as nearest to the scene, would not run down to Bar Harbor, look the situation over, and see what could be done."

I packed my bag and took the night train down, taking with me, in addition to the authority to act for the Directors, a letter from Dr. Robert Abbe, famous New York surgeon, who had been serving most efficiently the last few years as chairman of the Bar Harbor Village Improvement Association's sanitary committee and who denounced the project in no uncertain terms.

Arriving at the Ferry and taking the stout little steamboat which butted its way through the ice across the Upper Bay, I went directly on reaching Bar Harbor, to talk the matter over with the president of the Water Company, Mr. Fred C. Lynam. . . . His first reaction was that nothing could be done at that late stage to stop construction — the work had gone too far, and the cost would be too great. I then showed him Dr. Abbe's letter and told him of the instruction I had received from him to print it, were the project to go on. He read it and exclaimed: "For God's sake, don't print that letter!" I replied that I must, were construction to continue.

Finally it was settled that the summer resident for whom the house was being built should be communicated with to see whether, and upon what terms, he would consent to give the project up. . . . Found in Florida, he reluctantly gave the project up, the Company agreeing to repay him his expenditure upon the land, assuming the ownership and compensating the contractor.

Among Bar Harbor's rapidly increasing summer population there were, aside from Dr. Abbe, other physicians of national reputation. And at Seal Harbor resided Professor William T. Sedgwick of M.I.T., recognized as the first authority in America on sanitation. Dorr, realizing that he could count on the support of

From Beech Hill, Somesville, peering down on fresh water Echo Lake and beyond salt water Somes Sound.

many Mt. Desert taxpayers, entered a bill at Augusta and received the authority to condemn, on evidence of importance shown, the connected watersheds of Eagle Lake and Jordan Pond.

Possessed of new powers, Dorr was able, in the name of the Trustees, to purchase the Cedar Swamp Mountain spur, the amphitheatre between, the high slope of Sargent Mountain, and the grassy sward at the southern end of Jordan Pond.

At the beginning of 1913, Dorr was at home in Boston with every intention of spending a happy social winter there, particularly to enjoy pleasant sessions at the Atheneum and the Somerset Club. A telephone call came in from Harry Lynam in Bar Harbor, as Dorr tells in his privately printed *Acadia National Park, Its Origin and Background:*

The "Ravens Nest", Schoodic Point, Acadia National Park looking toward Mt. Desert Island.

Crude 'coys: coot and eider ducks on lobster pots at Wonsqueek Harbor by Acadia National Park, Schoodic side . . . called Wonsqueek because when an ancient brave drowned his squaw she gave but "one squeek" . . .

"Mr. Dorr, I think you will wish to know that a group of them down here have got together and have introduced a bill in the State Legislature, now convened at Augusta, to annul the charter of our Trustees of Public Reservations corporation."

Answering, I said: "I will take the train down to Augusta tonight. Meet me there tomorrow and we will see what can be done."

As it chanced, my friend, the Hon. John A. Peters of Ellsworth, was Speaker of the House that year. . . . He made me at home in his rooms at the hotel, where his friends and members of the House came to talk the business of the sessions over, and together, at other times, we went about ourselves and visited leading members who might have influence in our matter. In fact, we made a most thorough campaign of it, winning friends and votes so that when, ten days or so later, our bill came up for hearing the action of the committee on it was a foregone conclusion. . . .

Returning of a winter eve on the rails via Maine Central sleeper, Dorr lay awake, sleepless enough to decide categorically that some national protection must be effected to perpetuate the Mt. Desert lands. The U.S. Government must take under its wing the preserve he had so labored to assemble.

The train puffed at last into the bleakness of the North Station. Following a Boston breakfast, Dorr went straight to Cambridge to report to President Eliot on the danger that had threatened in Augusta. Eliot, of militant mind, at first believed that the Trustees should meet such attacks as they arose, as had been the policy of his unviersity in the face of Cambridge undertakings to tax its nonprofit lands and buildings. Dorr replied that the two cases were dissimilar, that "his" was in effect a one-man task, not comparable to Harvard, with its battalions of alumni. For example, if he himself had not been able and willing to drop everything and go to Augusta in the dead of winter, all would have been lost.

Eliot thought awhile and then said, "I believe you are right. When will you be going to Washington?"

"It is here," writes Dorr, "the story of our National Park begins, born of the attack upon our Public Reservations charter."

In a few weeks Dorr went on to Washington, his visit to coincide with the coming in of the new administration under President Wilson. He was welcomed by his host, Gifford Pinchot, Chief of the Forest Service and its founder under President Theodore Rosevelt. Dorr made a stay of some length in the capital, visiting friends, meeting important people, inquiring of one and another what was going on politically beneath the surface. Wilson's new policies were everywhere in the air; one could never tell what new acquaintance might benefit the Dorr quest. Remembered was a luncheon in honor of Secretary of the Treasury McAdoo and his bride, the President's daughter Eleanor, given al fresco at the Old Mill Restaurant in Rock Creek Park under a canopy of springtime, with music supplied by the full-flowing creek. The McAdoo contact was to serve Dorr well during ensuing trips to Washington.

At the end of the spring Dorr returned to Bar Harbor to gather together his papers, deeds, maps and titles and prepare for a return march on Washington.

There was no National Park Service at the time of Dorr's first visit. The act creating it was not passed until August 25, 1916. Yellowstone Park was still patrolled by U.S. Cavalry, and such parks as existed were cared for in various ways. Since the Congress was already loaded with bills for the establishment of National Parks, Dorr was advised by friends on the inside to take advantage of Theodore Roosevelt's 1906 National Monument Act, which gave the President powers to set aside by proclamation and place under federal control any tract of "exceptional historic . . . or scenic interist," and whose conservation should be recommended by the Secretary of War, Agriculture or Interior. A special clause, fortunately for Dorr, had been added to permit acquisitions from a private source.

Assuming President Eliot's and the Trustees' concurrence, Dorr decided on

Looking into the maw of Hall Quarry, Somes Sound, where eight hundred workmen once hewed granite blocks for the streets and buildings of American cities . . .

the spot to ask the government to accept the Mt. Desert tract in free gift as a National Monument. Acceptance now lay wholly with the President and on recommendation of authorized members of the Cabinet. Endorsement seemed assured, since Dorr knew he could count on the friendship of his good friend and cabinet officer Franklin K. Lane, Secretary of the Interior. Legal officials of the Public Lands Commission, taking their own sweet time, finally indicated on the maps submitted that two further tracts of land should be acquired to present a unit bounded by a single line. Secondly, more extensive study of the deeds and titles would be necessary to comply with the government's exacting standards.

More funds to expand further surveys, more exhausting study of the deeds! The Washington decision had been disappointing but not disheartening,

Egg Rock lighthouse, guidepost to Frenchman's Bay, is perched on a rocky island that is a favorite ambush for water fowlers at half tide ... Respectful authorities years ago veered the whistle's strident wails toward the open sea, thus sparing the sensitive eardrums of coastal neighbor, the aged publisher, Joseph Pulitzer I.

inasmuch as an expanded presentation led to so definite a gain. Dorr retreated to Bar Harbor and with Fred Lynam became immersed in the quest for deeds and grants, some extending back to the visits of the French landowners in the 1600's.

Not until the spring of 1916 — two years after Dorr's first offer had been made — did he feel justified in returning to Washington. Lynam had traced the copious legal records back to the earliest title of all, that of Antoine de la Mothe Cadillac, who obtained a grant from the Province of Quebec (confirmed by Louis XIV) which gave him, in true feudal style, the lordship (Seigneurie) of the *Isle des Monts-deserts*.

But Champlain had preceded Cadillac by more than eighty years: in 1604 the island's discoverer was sailing in the service of Sieur de Monts, a courtier of Henry of Navarre. It was the sponsor's name that Dorr affixed to his beloved project.

The deeds of the proposed Sieur de Monts Monument in their new comprehensive form were immediately approved in Washington. Now the offer of the Maine reservation lands would be addressed in due form to the Secretary of the Interior, the Honorable Franklin K. Lane, to forward to the President with his recommendation.

Days, then weeks went by. No answer from the White House on what had seemed mere routine. Dorr, by now champing at the bit, took action, and at the top.

Accompanied by Senator Johnson and Congressman Peters of Maine, he sought out the President and with the aid of photographs, explained his project; the Chief Executive seemed intrigued by the erudite Boston blueblood. The conversation hit an especially enthusiastic note when Dorr commended Wilson for his elevation of Justice Brandeis, Dorr's close Boston friend, to the Supreme

Hunter's Beach between Otter Creek and Seal Harbor.

Court, an appointment at the time bitterly opposed throughout most of the United States.

Dorr left the White House encouraged, but as empty weeks dragged on, discouragement engulfed him.

By this date it was early summer; Washington was its usual, stifling, humid self in an era preceding the general use of air conditioning. Would it not be opportune to invite the Wilsons to Oldfarm, where the President could view the intended Sieur de Monts Monument for himself?

Another of Dorr's good Boston friends, Charles Hamlin, Wilson's appointee to the governorship of the Federal Reserve Bank, arranged for a friendly call on Mrs. Wilson, who greeted the pair in the reception room of the White House. Dorr at once extended his invitation.

"But," she stammered — apparently she and her husband had discussed

(Left) Not a Japanese print by Hokusai, but Sand Beach, Bar Harbor, silhouetted against the autumn sun.

Dorr's project during lunch — "the President does not feel sure that he would be legally justified in signing that proclamation."

Without more ado than courtsey required, Dorr departed the White House for friends in the Department of Interior (Albright and Cotter) to tell them of Mrs. Wilson's cryptic remark. When he asked its meaning Dorr was told, "It means that the Forest Service has been knifing us!"

Next stop: across the street to the Forest Service, then occupying but a single suite of rooms in a building on F Street, to find Director Graves, once outspoken in favor of the Dorr project. Still of the same mind, Graves agreed this time to put his recommendation into writing. Calling in a stenographer, he dictated on the spot a warm approval. Dorr's call proved that Graves himself was in no way at fault, but events were to reveal that the friends in the Interior Department were, with their accusation, close to the truth.

A bewildered Dorr again sought out Senator Johnson. Maine's only Democratic senator in years, he was to come up for re-election in the following autumn, and recognition by the Federal Government of Maine's great coastal scenery would aid his cause. An indignant Johnson, who enjoyed particular influence at the White House, stormed the President's secretary, Joseph Tumulty, via the telephone. A Wilson and Johnson conference was quickly arranged.

Dorr waited for the senator outside the entrance to the Executive Chambers of the White House. When Johnson came out he said:

"I had a good talk with the President; I don't believe he'll turn us down! I gave him your papers showing the complete legality of what you ask, and that his own use of the Act out west upon more than one occasion had established a clear

104

The Ovens, Bar Harbor; striking geology at upper Frenchmans Bay, Salisbury Cove, where arched caves have developed in the face of a vertical cliff.

precedent. Then I said to him, 'Mr. President, I don't want you to turn this down!' He wasn't born yesterday; he knew what I meant!"

Still the proclamation did not come back. No word from either the President or Secretary Lane. Soon after, Dorr chanced to be dining at the Metropolitan Club when Governor Hamlin and Secretary McAdoo, who had been with a party at another table, came across the room to greet him.

"Mr. Dorr," said the president's son-in-law, "Governor Hamlin has been telling me what you are planning to create on the Maine coast and I want to tell you that I think it's splendid. If there is anything that I can do to help, I shall be glad to do it."

Dorr replied, "Just one thing. Find out for me at the White House what the difficulty is that President Wilson does not sign our proclamation."

As Dorr relates it:

> The next day at noon I was in the Governor's office in the Treasury Building, when Secretary McAdoo came in on his way back from a meeting of the Cabinet and said:
> "I've come to report!"
> His report was that Secretary Houston of the Department of Agriculture, who had at that time great influence with the President, had submitted a written memorandum in opposition to our plan.

Governor Hamlin, a close neighbor of Houston's in Washington who saw him intimately out of office hours, volunteered to take up the matter for Dorr. The latter told Hamlin that he had cared for these lands since they were acquired and would continue to do so, should the government accept, however long it might be till Congress should see fit to grant an appropriation.

Accordingly, Hamlin had his talk with Secretary Houston, and the question of funds did come up. The governor, prepared in advance, was ready to meet it. Secretary Houston then raised the objection that the government could not accept gratuitous service. This had occurred to Dorr, and again Governor Hamlin was prepared to say that Dorr would take over charge of the monument at the lowest salary paid at that time to anyone in government service — a dollar a month.

Frenchmans Bay Foreground Islands as seen from Mt. Cadillac, Bar Harbor. Left to right: Bar Island, Sheep Porcupine, Burnt Porcupine, Long Porcupine and Bald Porcupine.

PHOTO BY PAUL FAVOUR

Despite Hamlin's report, Dorr still believed prejudice might easily outweigh reason. He played a trump hand. Remembering that Secretary Houston, earlier in his academic career as a Harvard professor, had been indebted for kindness shown to him by the University, Dorr telegraphed President Eliot asking him to write the secretary in his own hand. The wire caught Eliot just as he was about to leave for Northeast Harbor; he sat down at once and wrote to Secretary Houston in a dry humor that could be evident only to Eliot and Dorr —

> Dear Secretary:
> I know this does not come within your province, but I cannot but feel that you will be interested to cooperate with Mr. Dorr and myself in what we believe to be so much for the public good. . .

— going on to outline, as though it were new to Secretary Houston, what they had hoped and planned.

Three days after receiving the letter, Secretary Houston, wrote President Wilson, "I have changed my view in regard to the proposed reservation on the coast of Maine and now think it highly desirable that you accept. . . . " Three days after he received this letter — July 8, 1916 — President Wilson signed the proclamation.

At last the monument had been established. The Dorr purse, once fathoms deep, had reached a shallow level; the buying up of the titles of mountain lands had offered few opportunities at discount prices. A national appropriation needed to be secured to keep the Park well groomed and protected. Since Dorr's bill had been signed after the beginning of the Government's fiscal year (following July 1, 1916), there was no appropriation of any nature. The following year its share was the princely amount of $150. Records show that Dorr expended this on "ranger service for wildlife and bird protection."

The director of the new Sieur de Monts Monument now made plans to leave for Chicago to get in touch with the Board of Trustees of the university, with whom Eliot, now President Emeritus of Harvard, had been consulting in the belief that he could thereby assist Dorr's "Wild Gardens" scheme for Acadia. Before departing for the Midwest, Dorr did his best to persuade Secretary Lane that he should come to Bar Harbor for a visit at Oldfarm and see the lands he had so vitally helped. But until the international situation changed to a definite pattern, Lane saw no hope for such a visit.

Arriving in Chicago, however, Dorr found a telegram from Secretary Lane saying that, after all, he and his wife would be able to come, arriving at Bar Harbor the morning of August 23rd. Dorr had just time to retrace his steps and connect with the Lane's night train in Portland. All was in readiness at Oldfarm. The visit was a great success. Lane, several years Dorr's junior, had a weak heart that made it unwise for him to climb Cadillac; with the old road nearly washed away, Dorr strode beside Lane's horse lest it slip on the ice-planed granite. But the ascent went well. Safely arrived at the summit, the Secretary of the Interior was wildly impressed with the great sweep of sea and land.

When the last day of the visit came, I asked the Secretary where he would best like to go and spend the morning, and he replied:

"I'd like to go again to your spring. What you have done there, with its broad human appeal and recollection of old scenes abroad, interests me more than anything else I have seen."

So to Sieur de Monts spring we went and strolled about. Alone for a moment with Mrs. Lane, I said to her:

"There's something I want to talk over with your husband before you go," and started to tell her what it was when he returned and asked:

"What are you two conspirators talking about?"

I answered: "I was telling Mrs. Lane that I had just got word from the Chief Clerk of your new National Park set-up in Washington instructing me, as custodian, to submit my estimate for the Monument this coming year. Having had as yet no appropriation to deal with, I have never submitted an estimate before and have no precedent to guide me. So I want to take advantage of your presence here and ask you, now that you have seen the Monument, to tell me what to ask for."

He thought for a moment, then said: "Fifty thousand dollars!"

The Chief Clerk of the new National Park Service had instructed me, in the letter I had received, that in making my estimate for the Monument, I should not at most exceed thirteen hundred and fifty dollars; this I had thought wiser not to tell the Secretary, but to let him decide the matter freely and without suggestion. So I simply replied:

"You as Secretary fo the Interior are the titular head of the National Park Service. I will write back and say that you have visited the Monument and seen our needs, have instructed me to ask for fifty thousand dollars." And so I did.

When Secretary Lane returned to Washington he held to his point in spite of remonstrance and the estimate he had set was entered.

Later that year, however, when Dorr returned to Washington, Mrs. Lane told him without ado, "I'm afraid it's no use!"

"Comprehending her meaning, I said: 'What is no use — to ask for the full amount that Secretary Lane instructed me to ask for, or to ask for anything at all?'"

" 'For anything at all,' she answered. 'Dining out the other day I sat next to Mr. Sherley and took the opportunity to take the matter up. He would not even listen to it, but said, "With the Nation at war, nothing new can be considered." ' "

The Honorable Swagar Sherley! A foreboding name with which to contend; Dorr must hurdle Representative Sherley of Kentucky, the autocratic, all-powerful head of the House Appropriations Committee. At that time there existed no Budget Committee to review and pass upon appropriations originating in the House.

Why give up without at least a trial? Secretary Lane, though admitting that any attempt to twist Sherley's arm was not sound procedure, acceded to the request of a desperate Dorr. Lane, and a dozen others who would be listened to on Capitol Hill, wrote directly to the austere chairman from Kentucky. But nothing seemed to give at any seam.

Seal Harbor's Little Long Pond. Not to be confused with the much greater Long Pond some ten miles distant near Somesville and the Western Mountains.

A few days later in New York, Dorr chanced to note in the paper that former president Theordore Roosevelt was in residence at Oyster Bay. Dorr knew him slightly, well enough to call him for a letter on the needed appropriation, but the telephone company would not give out the Roosevelt number. On the street the very next day, Door bumped into Mrs. Douglas Robinson, the Colonel's sister. Of course she would give him her brother's number. Better still, Colonel Roosevelt was to lunch at the Colony Club with Mrs. Woolcott, widow of the former Senator from Colorado.

"Ask yourself to the luncheon," advised Mrs. Robinson. Dorr had no compunctions about this, and the assignation was arranged. Some years before in Rome, Dorr had performed a considerable favor for Mrs. Woolcott.

Dorr came in at dessert and went away with T. R. in the Colonel's car. A few days later a Roosevelt note arrived, enclosing a copy of the letter the Colonel had written to Sherley:

April 10, 1918

My dear Mr. Sherley:

As a man who has been deeply interested for years in the growth and development of our National Park System, I respectfully urge on your Committee favorable action on Secretary Lane's request for adequate appropriation for the Sieur de Monts National Monument on the coast of Maine. It is our one eastern national park and gives for the first time to the crowded

At right: Penobscot Mountain set in a network of foot trails. The island offers paths for all types of trampers, the spectacular climber or the leisurely pedestrian.

Below: Balanced Boulder On South Bubble Mountain Glamourous Jordan Pond Road below. Beyond is open sea, Seal Harbor, and outer islands: two Cranberries, Bakers, Suttons, Greenings, and the two Ducks.

eastern city population of the country the opportunity to share directly and immediately in our national park system.

Its striking ocean frontage makes it unlike any other we have, and I have watched with keen interest the work that has led to its creation. Under the right development it will furnish a health-giving playground, greatly needed, to multitudes of hard-working men and women; it constitutes also a wild life sanctuary under national guardianship at a point where such a sanctuary is greatly needed.

Secretary Lane's request for adequate provision for this park is in accordance with the broad national policy for the conservation and development of our home resources — a policy which every year becomes of increasing consequence.

Faithfully yours,
THEODORE ROOSEVELT

A few days later came a copy of Sherley's reply to Colonel Roosevelt.

Dear Colonel Roosevelt;
I have your letter about the National Monument on the coast of Maine. We cannot at this time, with the Nation at war, do what we would at another, but I think I can assure you that an appropriation will be made.

Truly yours,
SWAGAR SHERLEY

The T. R. letter had broken the log jam. When the Appropriations Committee bill came out, the amount of $10,000 was allotted to the Monument, accompanied by the statement that because the tract was truly one of National Park characteristics it should be made into a National Park. This provided Dorr with the opportunity he had been seeking — his next and final step. For this, congressional action would be required, and if it was to be obtained in the current session, there was no time to lose.

Dorr's helpful friend, now Representative Peters of Maine, was serving his first term in Congress. He and Senator Hale, who entered Dorr's bill, were of the greatest assistance.

"At that time," Dorr relates, "I planned to call the Park the Mount Desert National Park. But at the hearing held when its time came by the Public Lands Committee of the House — one of some size and wholly composed, as it chanced, of western men — someone asked what the name meant. Was it really a desert?

I had to explain that in the old French meaning of the word, in Champlain's time, the word "desert" meant uninhabited by man, wild but not devoid of life.
Then another asked, "Where is it?"
And I realized I had counted too much on the knowledge of our coast and Island the country over. This caused me to reflect. The name I had taken for the Monument, that of Sieur de Monts, I would have liked to use but found it difficult of pronunciation for Americans not versed in French. So I took the matter up

with Senator Hale, whose bill it still remained, and told him of my experience, saying:

"It would be of interest to tie up the Park's creation, in naming it, with the great events of the period of the war in Frnace."

"Then," said he, "the name to take is Lafayette."

That was a time when the whole east was taking the war in the spirit of a high crusade and Lafayette's name was foremost in men's thoughts. After consulting with President Eliot and Congressman Peters, that name was taken, and Lafayette National Park it became and remained for the next ten years.

The Public Lands Committee reported favorably. A single objection could have thrown it out of the Unanimous Consent Calendar, but it was gavelled through 1-2-3, aided by the Speaker of the House, Frederick Gillette of Massachusetts, another old Dorr acquaintance. The bill now passed rapidly through the routine stages of its further progress, to the desk of the President of the Senate and, in due course, to the executive chambers of the White House for President Wilson's signature.

There was but little time to gain the Wilson signature. The signing of the President of the Senate was a mere formality. Along with the Acadia bill, Dorr, now at confident cruising speed, obtained on behalf of Director Mather of the National Park Service the signature for another bill, which would change the Grand Canyon National Monument in Arizona into a National Park. Entrusted with both bills, Dorr, as a special messenger, made haste to the executive chambers of the White House, where he explained to Woodrow Wilson's secretary the need for the President's signature that very night. Conscious of the pressure caused by the President's brief return and fearful that the two bills might rest on his desk unsigned, Dorr purchased two fountain pens of the best make, filled them with ink and pleaded with the secretary to be sure that Wilson used one to sign each of the bills. As night came on, he sat down and waited.

Then a call came from the President's secretary; Dorr learned with dismay that the bills still needed the endorsement of the Secretary of the Interior. The new offices of the Interior Department were but a step away, and luckily Secretary Lane, himself busy over the President's return, was working late. Dorr caught him as he left for home and returned, the signed bills in hand, to the executive chambers.

Let Dorr's own words close the description of this important moment in his life:

The President worked that first, and as it proved single, day at Washington — that of February 26th, 1919 — on his return from France late into the night. A friendly assistant secretary whom I had interested in our need, watching his opportunity, laid our bills before him, got his signature, and started them on the way into the record before I left. The task that I had set myself to do six years before was done.

Early in the game George B. Dorr must have learned that it is difficult without imagination, energy, tact and money to fight City Hall, or, for that matter,

Upper Hadlock Pond, Northeast Harbor and majestic Sargent Mountain, one peak that outlasted the change of names with the establishment of the Park.

prejudice among rich and poor. While hewing to his ideas and ideals for a National Park, he often had to retreat one step to accomplish two forward. With this "If you can't lick 'em, join 'em" philosophy he countered two threats to the pastoral sublimity of his beautiful Mt. Desert Island.

One morning in 1907, Dorr's Boston mail contained a bulging letter from John S. Kennedy in New York. The banker had come upon the intelligence that a group of Boston speculators had combined with Southwest Harbor fishermen in a plan to transport their salt fish by a trolley line which, if built, would extend to the Maine Central tracks at Ellsworth. If a state charter could be obtained, this would allow a trolley line to pass over the main driving road — horseless carriages were then excluded — from Ellsworth to Bar Harbor, with a branch through Somesville to Southwest.

Dorr at once replied to Mr. Kennedy, and to the equally interested Clement A. Newbold of Philadelphia and Northeast Harbor, that he most certainly would take steps to protect the isolation of the island. Nonetheless he foresaw that his approach would need to be tempered with tolerance and a sense of oncoming events. As the night the day, an increasing development of the automobile would

114

soon be accompanied by an ever rising tide of tourists. The best way to neutralize the situation would be to strike first. He would project his own plans for an electric line; so controlled, it would scar the landscape as little as possible. Such a trolley would proceed down the Union River to cross the Narrows by its own bridge, then cut deeply through the woods and marshlands of the island to Bar Harbor, with the necessary branch to Southwest.

With such a plan in mind, Dorr consented to come down from Boston and meet with the petitioners at John A. Peters' house in Ellsworth.

> The meeting duly arranged [he writes], I took the night train down from Boston. To breathe the morning air and stretch my legs, I got off the train at Bangor at dawn, not waiting to put on my overcoat. The Station Master coming by swinging his lantern, I remarked:
>
> "It's a cold day!"
>
> "Thirty-eight," he answered and went on his way. This was thirty-eight below zero, the coldest, it chanced, that I had ever till then experienced. But the air was dry and, putting my hands in my pockets, I continued strolling up and down the platform till the train whistled in signal that it was ready to go.
>
> At Ellsworth, when I had reached Mr. Peters' warm and comfortable house, it was still far below. Our meeting went off well. The fishing folk at Southwest agreed to withdraw their application for a charter on my pledging our intended corporation to a real study of the problem. . . . Without the support of the Southwest Harbor fishing interests there would be no chance the Legislature would grant a charter to outside interests, not demanded by the people of the region. And there the matter rested. . . .

That afternoon Dorr's caretaker drove him over to Bar Harbor behind a fast horse in an open sleigh, with a buffalo robe for warmth. The sparkling twenty-five-mile ride terminated at the welcoming lights of Oldfarm; within, the comfortable atmosphere glowed from the crackling logs of several open fireplaces. The outside temperature, though mitigated by the sea, was still sixteen below.

In the cold of the next morning, before word could get about, Dorr made arrangements to take options simultaneously, should the railroad be built, on certain strategic points from Bar Harbor to Southwest. During the following spring and through the fall, two crews of surveyors made a thorough study of the best routes over grades whereby electric power could be generated at less than half the necessary standby charge. The elevations over the Bluffs at Bar Harbor compelled long, high-cost circuits and an exhaustive electric power throughout the line, so much as to render impossible economic operation. The Southwest fathers, who had followed the work with interest, were satisfied that Dorr had done the best for them that could be done. Mission accomplished — tactfully, expensively, but the victory won.

Ten years later, the long-pigeonholed plans for Dorr's unborn electric road had a day in court. By this time, 1911, a number of year-round Bar Harbor residents were petitioning for repeal of a law passed some years before by the Maine Legislature forbidding all use on the island of the crude motor cars of the time. In

The Tarn, below Dorr Mountain on the road from Bar Harbor to Otter Creek and Seal Harbor. Dictionary defines 'tarn' as a "small mountain lake."

1907 they had lost out with a similar protest when a committee of summer folk, having mounted a liberal fund, applied it with some eyebrow-raising methods in the purlieus of Augusta, where, as it was stated, "it would do the most good."

Dorr realized full well that with improved automobiles making great strides throughout the United States and given free access across the rest of Maine, a fresh attempt to get the law repealed might very well succeed. Could the change — which he saw as inevitable in the end — be brought about gradually, and with deliberate speed? Then he remembered the unused blueprints for the electric roadbed.

Prominent and profitable features of Bar Harbor were the fine trotting horses owned by the residents. These and other equine classes appeared frequently at the racetrack and horse-show ring owned by Edward Morrell of Philadelphia under Champlain Mountain; the area, today marked by a bronze tablet, lies just below the Jackson Laboratory on the road near Sieur de Monts Spring. Supplying the appurtenances of the horse in the form of tack, buckboards and cut-unders was one of the chief industries of the town. The livery-stable business offered a good living, Dorr reasoned, that would be lost to many local

116

Somes Sound from the Sargeant Drive. Samuel Duncan Sargeant (but no relation to Sargent Mountain) was a leader in preserving and disclosing the beauty of the island. Somes is the only true fjord on USA's Atlantic Coast. Depth in one place is 165 feet.

people were automobiles brought in. Why not an automobile road over the old course of the abandoned electric road? This would enable distant motorists to reach Bar Harbor with their own cars, but once there they must use horses. The idea went too far for some, not far enough for others. Dorr was again under fire from summer residents and townspeople alike.

As chairman of the committee opposing automobiles, C. Ledyard Blair — the same adroit hand who would later pilot the *Kronprizessin Cecilie* up Frenchman's Bay to a safe anchorage at Bar Harbor — called a meeting of Mt. Desert residents at his house in New York. Few shared Dorr's view that automobiles were sure to come.

"Mr. Blair," said Dorr, "when the question of opening the Island to automobiles first came up two years ago and your committee was formed to defeat it, it was able to do so, but not without the employment of a substantial fund whose raising and expenditure incurred no little criticism. Since then the use and development of the automobile has come on apace the country over and the difficulties of keeping them off the Island will be correspondingly greater. How do you propose to defeat it now?"

"Defeat it any way we can," he answered. At this, William Lee, Dorr's friend and neighbor at Bar Harbor, was taken aback and exclaimed, "Oh, Mr. Blair, you don't mean that!" But Blair did.

The Legislature hearing on the question, at Augusta in January, was held before the Judiciary Committee and an unprecedented audience. Bar Harbor's own Judge Deasy, the clever, urbane, much respected native son and senior partner of Deasy, Lynam, Rodick & Rodick, opened the arguments for a now tempered summer group, whose arbitrary demands for total automobile ban had been watered down by the shrewd, patient negotiations of George Dorr. Deasy was opposed by William Sherman, Town Clerk and stationer at Bar Harbor and

Representative to the State Legislature, who now led a militant townfolk seeking to repeal the existing prohibition on automobiles.

Deasy, fortified with Dorr's compromise road plan, gained an initial advantage by bringing forth the old electric-line surveys, offering a constructive solution against the town's more drastic bill, which called for immediate action.

Dorr relates the amusing exchange:

> [Deasy] had got hold of a publication sold by Mr. Sherman at his stationery shop, which, published as a guide to Bar Harbor, bore his name. In it was stated that one of the chief assets of the town as a resort was its picturesque, exciting drives "skirting the edge of precipitous cliffs, descending into deep ravines, rasing up to heights with glorious views. . . . " From this Mr. Deasy read such portions as were suited to his purpose and ended by asking:
>
> "Now, Gentlemen, do you consider this a suitable place to open to these dangerous contraptions?"
>
> Mr. Sherman, a most excellent man and valuable citizen, but of a naturally nervous and excitable temperament, was unable at this point to control his feelings and sprang to his feet, exclaiming to the Committee:
>
> "Gentlemen, I protest!"
>
> Mr. Deasy, breaking off his reading and looking down his spectacles at Mr. Sherman, asked, with the book he had been reading from in his hand:
>
> "Mr. Sherman, is not this your writing?"
>
> "No!" shouted Mr. Sherman.
>
> "Why," continued Mr. Deasy, "it bears your name. Do you mean to say that you put your name to what you do not write?"
>
> Here the chairman of the Committee interrupted to say, "Mr. Sherman, you are out of order; you will please resume your seat."
>
> Mr. Sherman reluctantly sat down, while Mr. Deasy continued his reading from the pamphlet, commenting on it to the Committee as he read. But soon this proved more than Mr. Sherman could endure, and he rose again to speak in further protest when the chairman peremptorily ordered him to resume his seat — he would be given his opportunity later, he said, to present his side of the case.

Deasy's forensic brilliance, based on Dorr's creative proposal, achieved the net result of a two-year postponement of the admittance of automobiles to the town. The Dorr compromise assuaged a few, but not many, of the summer residents. The local people, particularly in the horse-livery group, had time to make adjustments. Two years later, in 1915, Seal and Northeast Harbors removed their bans. Nevertheless, the acceptance of the automobile, *pro bono publico,* represented the end of a Mt. Desert era.

One gentleman of Seal Harbor who had arrived at the island the summer of 1900 would react impressively to the admittance of automobiles. This was none other than John D. Rockefeller, Jr., who on sight had become enamored of the distinctive forests, backing up this early endearment by copious purchases of real estate. It was his positive enjoyment to ride forth on the wooded byways.

The building of roads was a family passion. Tarrytown, New York, seat of the Rockefeller clan, was honeycombed with do-it-yourself thoroughfares; one

Northeast Harbor lady, not overly enthusiastic at Rockefeller's Caesar-like road building, referred to the New York estate as "a huge waffle iron." Henceforth on Mt. Desert, for his own and his neighbor's use, Mr. Rockefeller would construct a plethora of automobile-free roads, sylvan avenues of lasting beauty.

The great philanthropist, who was to become as valuabe to the Dorr cause as John Stewart Kennedy had ever been, found his plans blocked at the upper end of Little Long Pond, a picturesque area lying beyond an exquisite curve in the Shore Road between Seal and Northeast Harbors: the desired land already belonged to the Trustees of Hancock County Public Reservations. Would the Trustees sell the land at the inland base of the tiny lake? Yes, came back the eventual reply, if Mr. Rockefeller would take his chance with the United States Government — should the land pass into its eventual ownership — and contingent on continued restriction to horse use. The offer was accepted.

During the ensuing years a seemingly close friendship grew up between George Dorr and Rockefeller. In 1917, while the Sieur de Monts Monument was continuing apace under its dollar-a-month director, Dorr was honored by a visit from his Washington superior, Secretary of the Interior Franklin K. Lane. Dorr arranged for Lane to lunch with Rockefeller, at which time the latter presented to the secretary a grandiose plan for an extended road system with superbly designed bridges and overpasses, to be constructed partly on his own land and partly on land which now belonged to the government. Lane personally gave his permission.

The Rockefeller road crew swung into action and, for a period of almost three years, interlaced the new Park with driving roads. These were concealed from the public highways, but to the inquisitive tramper they opened up exciting vistas deep in the forests that few knew existed. The current set of projected roads were finished, save one. This was to circle around the Amphitheatre Valley between the two branches into which Jordan (Penobscot) Mountain divides — Cedar Swamp and Lower Jordan — and continue around the latter's southern end.

The bulldozers were moving into formation for an attack on the last assignment. Then, one June morning in 1920, Mr. Rockefeller motored over to Oldfarm with a letter he had received from George Wharton Pepper of Philadelphia and Northeast Harbor. It began by commending him for the roads he had completed and thanking him for the pleasure they had given, but it ended with the request that he build no more: apparently the road as yet unbuilt was to come a little too close to the sacred atmosphere of Northeast.

Pepper — famous Philadelphia lawyer and a civic leader unused to having his will disputed — had, it seemed, been unwilling to envision that the new landscaped roads would ever blend into the natural camouflage of the woods. Dorr never lost his urbanity in his exchanges with Pepper. Probably he realized he was up against sterling silver, opposed by a man who, in his way, loved Mt. Desert Island as much as Dorr himself, attempting to keep it inviolate not only for Pepper but for his Philadelphia neighbors as well. For in the words of Nathaniel

Burt, Philadelphians "go swarming in summer where other Philadelphians swarm."

To sound out Northeast Harbor summer sentiment before taking action on the burning question, Lincoln Cromwell of New York, president of the Northeast Harbor Village Improvement Association, called together a small group, a dozen or more, at his house. Dorr was asked as the representative of the government.

Pepper was in full cry concerning the disfigurement caused by the Rockefeller roads. Dorr took issue with him, insisting that these wooded pathways, rightly planned, would supplement harmoniously the virgin forest through which they passed. Some lines from Milton seemed to fit the moment:

> *Thick as autumnal leaves that strow the brooks*
> *In Vallombrosa, where th' Etrurian shades*
> *High over-arch'd imbower.*

A few days later Dorr received a letter from Pepper, saying, "When you quoted Milton, I knew my cause was lost." But it was not lost, for as the result of Pepper's opposition in which others joined, Mr. Rockefeller ceased construction. Later, when Pepper had become U.S. Senator, Dorr and he would again cross swords. Dorr meanwhile had not lost the Rockefeller backing, nor had Rockefeller lost the urge to build roads.

Dorr needed a simple woods thoroughfare over which his few rangers could pass readily between the northern and southern side of the Park mountain range. This wish was soon answered from Seal Harbor, and in expanded form. A second Dorr suggestion was to outline the benefits of a horse road along the western side of Jordan Pond to connect with existing trails below the Bubbles, looking down on Eagle Lake. Not only this but other connecting systems were offered by Mr. Rockefeller, including an offer of $150,000 for construction of the first Park automobile road — which, or course, saw eventual completion as the glamorous eighteen-mile-an-hour road (the original speed limit). After ten at night a chain barred motorists from both ends, at the base of Cadillac and at the Jordan Pond House.

The package offer — a system of horse roads and a motor road — Mr. Rockefeller regarded as a unit, to be accepted or declined as such. Dorr forwarded the presentation to the National Park Service in the fall of 1921 with the recommendation that it be accepted. The top directors of the service came to assess the new proposal and seconded the recommendation.

Mr. Rockefeller went ahead with his beloved horse roads; Dorr, in the fall of 1923, started work on the Bar Harbor-to-Jordan Pond road, to become one of the most entrancing brief motor rides in the United States. Since the way lay mostly over bare, glaciated rock, with no soil to freeze, work could proceed in winter.

Now George Wharton Pepper, newly elected Senator to fill the *ad interim* term of Boies Penrose, rose again in opposition, this time throwing his weight from Washington. Dorr proceeded to show the Philadelphian how politics could offer fair play, even to amateurs.

Pepper had applied pressure on Park authorities to have all work stopped on Dorr's public road. Dorr reminded Arno B. Cammerer, assistant director of the National Park Service, that since his crew had been chosen for a whole winter's job, and because of the importance of the names involved, no power on earth could prevent the negating of the assignment from being a front-page story. Back came a telegram to continue the work in progress, but to come immediately to Washington for a hearing.

On arriving at the capital, Dorr learned the essence of the scuttlebutt. The executive secretary of the National Parks Association, Robert Sterling Yard,* had been approached by Senator Pepper and Harold Peabody, chairman of the Path Committee of Bar Harbor; in Yard's office, Pepper had bitterly attacked the Rockefeller roads to the point of threatening to condemn them from the floor of the Senate. There, of course, he would speak under privilege; no opportunity would exist to rebut what he might say. Meanwhile, Pepper had bent the ear of Secretary Work of the Department of the Interior. The latter, duly impressed by the senatorial intensity, ordered all work stopped until he could mount an investigation.

Dorr made sure that the hearing was delayed long enough (till March 24) for him to organize a defense. He now pulled a new rabbit out of the hat, letting the State of Maine politicos in on a secret — a proposed spectacular drive up Mt. Cadillac. What plum would he come up with next? Dorr found no difficulty in obtaining support in the *affaire* Pepper; the whole state was with him. When the hearing convened, he was on hand with a strong delegation: the Governor, the State Forestry Service, political organizations and a sprinkling of summer residents.

It happened to be an election year. President Coolidge was running for his second term; Senator Pepper wanted to make the "keynote" speech in Maine. He was politely alerted by Dorr's delegation that if he were to oppose the state's resort-development interests, he would not be welcome as a speaker.

Pepper arose; apparently the message had gotten through. The previous acerbity seemed suddenly to have departed from him. His remarks concerning Dorr appeared more complimentary than critical. However Chairman Peabody of the Path Committee would have his say, centering his attack on work done by Mr. Rockefeller in the construction of his horse road system, particularly the thoroughfare around the basin of Upper Hadlock Pond (actually Northeast Harbor territory), where two major bridges had been built.

Peabody retained the floor for several minutes. Dorr, letting him have his say, waited quietly until he was done. Then the tall director of Lafayette National

---

*Secretary Yard once visited Oldfarm at a time when household help was in short supply. The word was passed along to Bar Harbor's Colonel Haskell H. Cleaves, then a West Point cadet on summer leave and in the employ of the Park, to report to the Dorr house for K. P. duty. Young Cleaves was involved in a lengthy session of shelling peas when an order came to secure the pea detail, to change immediately to his cadet's dress uniform and return on the double to act as escort for the young Miss Yard, who had just arrived with her parents.

View from Bernard looking toward Bass Harbor. Fishing villages predominate on the western side of Island.

Park arose, observing simply that there must be some misapprehension in Mr. Peabody's mind concerning the work Mr. Rockefeller had begun around the Hadlock Pond basin. None of that area lay within the Park: all was private property, owned by Mr. Rockefeller, and lay wholly outside the hearing's scope.

Secretary Work announced diplomatically that he would postpone decision till the following summer, when he could visit Bar Harbor and see the construction himself. Meanwhile, he directed that all commitments currently entered into would continue.

The next August, Work paid a call on President Coolidge in Massachusetts and then motored on to Bar Harbor. Dorr arranged to have Mrs. Henry F. Dimock, a celebrated Washington hostess, put up the Secretary and give one of her ponderous dinners in his honor; the next morning she returned him to Dorr for a look at Mr. Rockefeller's construction. Work kept to his comfortable car the entire trip over the island, refusing any pursuance of deep retreats in an available horsedrawn vehicle. His interests were political, and nature entered into them but little. He left for Washington that afternoon and the road building continued as before, but he enunciated that no new roads were to be constructed in the Park.

The next Rockefeller project extended over the Eagle Lake watershed lands that Dorr had, for good reason, not yet turned over to the Park but kept in the portfoilo of the Trustees of Public Reservations of Hancock County. The new venture would entail an underpass at McFarland's Hill, Bar Harbor, the road above eventually leading to the Bluffs, giving Mr. Rockefeller's horse-road system a magnificent northern terminus and extending it from shore to shore.

122

Peabody appeared again as watchdog. Indignantly he wrote Secretary Work that, in spite of the secretary's instructions, a new road was being built along the western shore of Eagle Lake. The National Park Service sent the letter on to Dorr, who replied that the road in question lay quite outside Park domain, neither the government nor the secretary having any jurisdiction over it. Further queries from Peabody to the Secretary of the Interior were always forwarded to Dorr; so far as the Government was concerned, the matter was ended. Mr. Rockefeller proceeded with his work.

Dorr was now in his seventieth year and still the much-desired extra man for dinner. His next large acquisition would stem, in fact, from one particular evening of dining out. An invitation to exciting new lands would lead him off the island and across broad waters. Target: the majestic Schoodic Peninsula, a storm-beaten point at the upper jaw of wide Frenchman Bay.

Few realize that Schoodic became a Park possession before the annexation of the popular Ocean Drive-Otter Cliffs compound at Bar Harbor. The Schoodic transaction would bring about the change of name from Lafayette to Acadia National Park.

What was to be a six-year quest dated from a cool evening in early September, 1922; Dorr was dining at the Jordan Pond House, situated in the woods above Seal Harbor and famous since the turn of the century. Centered in the Park, it is nostalgically remembered for its white birchbark walls and generally rustic atmosphere, and especially for tea taken in the open to the accompaniment of idyllic popovers and jam. The little Swiss lake of Jordan Pond lies at the end of a grassy meadow below, bracketed by Sargent Mountain and the Bubbles.

Among the guests that evening, dining inside, were Mr. and Mrs. Warner M. Leeds, distant neighbors of Dorr on the shore at Bar Harbor. Dorr found himself seated next to Mrs. Leeds, and the conversation revolved around the favorite

Idle days at Jordan Pond.

Schoodic Point, outpost of Acadia National Park at the wide upper jaw of Frenchmans Bay across from Bar Harbor, a granite headland extending farther out into the U.S. Atlantic than any other eastern promontory. Positioned in the path of the rising sun is the familiar lobster boat, steadying sail set.

subject of the Boston bachelor. Before the repast had ended, Mrs. Leeds asked if he would not like to have her one-third interest in Schoodic Peninsula for his Trustees of Public Reservations.

Dorr knew the area well, having cruised its waters many times in a sailboat and, in earlier days, climbed its great headland for the spectacular views. Indeed, he would love to have it, he told his dinner partner.

Before marrying Mr. Leeds, she had been Mrs. John C. Moore of New York and Winter Harbor. Moore was largely responsible for building up Winter Harbor as a coastal summer resort; he was a native son of the area, having been born in Steuben. In Horatio Alger fashion, he had founded a successful brokerage house in Manhattan. His fortune made, he returned to develop the region, where his acquisitions included Schoodic. He hoped to hold the peninsula as wild park land; then, in the midst of planning and construction, he died. Schoodic was left in equal portions to his widow and two daughters.

Not long after making Dorr her offer, Mrs. Leeds went to Europe. Both Moore daughters were living in England; she hoped they would share in giving the Schoodic tract in their father's memory. Suddenly, Mrs. Leeds died, her interest in the property remaining in her estate. Mr. Leeds, an executor of his wife's property, was, Dorr tells us, "of thrifty nature." He now offered his wife's intended gift for sale to the Trustees of Public Reservations.

Failure to acquire the elusive third would have cost the free gift of the remaining two-thirds interest, which by now Dorr had secured conditionally from Lady Lee (formerly Miss Moore) and her unmarried sister in England. But thanks to Dorr's patience and tact, the Trustees did secure Schoodic Head, as Mrs. Leeds had intended; soon after came the opportunity to establish there the most powerful and sensitive overseas radio station on the Atlantic coast. Eventually, Schoodic would become a segment of the Park, but first the name of Lafayette, chosen for Francophile reasons in World War I, must be changed. The Moore sisters, now devoted to all things British, had objected to the old title.

Dorr chose "Acadia" — a name, incidentally, he had always thought would be more fitting. In the mind of the old scholar lingered the ghosts of French explorers, and visions of the lilies of France. But to apply the new name officially, and to enlarge the Park charter to make it subject for acquisitions throughout Hancock County, would require an Act of Congress, a procedure by now child's play to Dorr. Included with the bill, entered by the Hon. John E. Nelson of Augusta, was a proviso to make the Homans House an official guest house for Park administrators and other visiting dignitaries, and to provide for alterations and repairs to the old manse (acquired in 1924 upon the death of Mrs. Charles D. Homans of Boston, an old friend of the Dorr family and President Eliot).

Congressman Cramton of Michigan, Chairman of the Appropriations Committee for the Department of the Interior, had spent three days with his wife as guests of Dorr following a Canadian vacation and had warm memories of his charm and hospitality. In Washington he would back Dorr's new mission.

Cramton was working in his office at the Capitol on the last day of details for his Appropriations Bill when Dorr rushed in with his Schoodic data, and estimates for the refurbishing of Homans House. "You're just in time!" said Cramton. "Tomorrow my bill will close, and in another day you would have been too late."

Another photo finish for Dorr: the Cramton Committee acted favorably, entering Dorr's material into the Appropriations Bill less than an hour before its closing.

"And," wrote Dorr, "my difficulties were over. Acadia National Park acquired at once its Guest House and its name."

President Eliot in the spring of 1926 hoped he might be able to reach Northeast Harbor again, a wish that was to be realized. But his energy, already greatly reduced, continued to ebb. During July he joyously planned a future short cruise in the *Hearty*, but by August he no longer spoke of going on the water. Writes his biographer, Henry James;* "His hours were spent in his own house, and on the veranda. Sweet summer airs blew through the open windows and doors and brought him the odors of the fir trees, and of the beeches and the tide. If the day was foggy, a log fire burned on the hearth . . . . Then came days when he was content to keep to his bed."

The end came on August 22. "The Chief Citizen of the Republic" had lived ninety-two full years. He had spent the last forty-six summers (with the exception of one in Europe) on the Mt. Desert location recommended in 1880 by his beloved son — so much accomplished at his hand and so much to endure, including the unblemished preserve on Mt. Desert (as well as on majestic Schoodic), lands that he worshiped, now perpetuated by the persistent labors of his appointed disciple, George B. Dorr.

A preamble to the founding of the radio station on Schoodic must include the usual hassle of objections and last-minute signings. Again Mr. Rockefeller's wishes were debated and delayed; but this time it was the U.S. Navy who made his life, and Dorr's, exceedingly difficult.

March 1929, a half-year away from the Wall Street crash, found Dorr in Washington, staying with a fellow citizen of Bar Harbor, Gist Blair, in historic Blair House on Pennsylvania Avenue. Blair brought up the future of the spectacular land that encompassed not only the approach to Sand Beach but the massive shoreline slabs and spruces bracketing Thunder Hole, which led in pink granite to the rugged Otter Cliffs promontory. This wonderland had come by inheritance to an old Bar Harbor family, who now wished to divest themselves of it; tragedy if it fell into the wrong hands! Blair had taken a six-month option on the large panorama, hoping to raise the purchase price among Bar Harbor residents, but despite the plush times nothing in the way of clinking coin shook loose. The reliable Rockefeller purse, however, once more made its lovely sound. Mr. R. closed the deal via the Blair option and simultaneously purchased the bold, projecting pinnacle of Otter Cliff. This consummate act signaled Dorr's hopes that. Mr. Rockefeller would develop these fairest of acres as a unit for the public benefit, turning them over ultimately to Acadia National Park.

It seems surprising that the so-called Ocean Drive frontage — the line of striking granite coastline between Sand Beach and Otter Point had not already fallen to the Trustees or to the Park. How had it escaped those avid collector parlays — Dorr and Kennedy, and later Dorr and Rockefeller, both entries on a hard drive since 1901?

At the beginning of the 1930's, surveyors and engineers had their plans complete and Mr. Rockefeller submitted to Washington a stupendous project, including a continuous Acadia Park motor road that would connect the Cadillac

---

*This Henry James, son of William the philosopher and nephew of Henry the novelist, won the Pulitzer Prize for his two-volume biography of Eliot.

PHOTO BY W. H. BALLARD

Bass Harbor Head looking inboard.

Mountain road unbrokenly with the ocean perimeter. Two horse roads were thrown in, further embellishing his extensive gravel network through the forests.

A map setting forth the offer was sent down to Bar Harbor from Washington, to occupy a wall in the Acadia Park office. No sooner posted and exposed to public view it blew up a storm more bitter, if possible, than the Philadelphia pepper pot of 1924. But now a sophisticated Department of the Interior, supported by the National Park Service, gave little heed to the vested summer interests and forthwith accepted Mr. Rockefeller's princely offer.

And by this time Mr. Rockefeller's inhibitions were disappearing. He could be proud when, like Cortez, he surveyed his Park gift domains, undeniably majestic — rustic roads edged with fast-growing cover, mountain motor courses bordered with pink granite, superbly engineered stone bridges molding softly into the enveloping forests. He recommended work on the Amphitheatre Road begun twelve years before, whose construction he had withdrawn in deference to Pepper and his friends but which he now felt to be essential to his horse-road system.

Work, of course, was to begin on the lengthy Ocean Drive reconstruction, which the town of Bar Harbor at its annual March meeting had turned over to the Park in support of the Rockefeller aim. Progress was delayed, however, pending removal of obstacles presented by the conditions accompanying Mr. Rockefeller's offer. Of these the most difficult to resolve was the Otter Cliffs Naval Station, which he insisted be moved if there were to be any coastal drive: to this the equivalent of today's Pentagon raised stern objection. An impasse followed which lasted all summer. The National Park Service was becoming discouraged; meanwhile, the time limit set by Mr. Rockefeller for fulfilling the obligation was drawing near. As Dorr puts it, "A magnificent coastal drive, of inestimable value to the future, hung in the balance; to secure it we must act without delay." A familiar call!

The Otter Cliffs station, developed in response to a World War I emergency, had proved so excellent a receiving location that it was used exclusively thereafter during President Wilson's stay abroad for his Washington communications. Dorr knew that any site less favorable would, in exchange, be unacceptable to the Navy Department, But he believed there was one place that might equal it — the projection far seaward of Schoodic Peninsula, the Park's recent acquisition.

From Boston, the First Naval District's Admiral Andrews gave his endorsement. Surveys were made, water was drilled for and found, the National Park Service in the person of Director Horace M. Albright viewed the scene. Harvard sent scientists to prove, via a temporary aerial, the ease of receiving communications from everywhere, even Australia and Japan. (The last, they believed, had come via the North Pole.) This twenty-four-hour vigil in a rough ranger's cabin proved that there could be no question of the exceptional radio receptiveness of the Schoodic site. Objection could center only on its relative isolation for Navy personnel, or the absence of a good road connection.

When in doubt, the politicians! Former Congressman Peters of Ellsworth was now Judge Peters; Dorr took up the matter through him and with Maine's

Rear of Bass Harbor Lighthouse . . . . the winter wind in the woolens. Offshore a can buoy marks the channel current.

Senator Hale, the chairman of the Senate Naval Committee. He also enlisted the help of Representative John E. Nelson of Augusta.

The Secretary of the Navy, an old Boston friend whom Dorr called Charles Francis Adams the younger, though well disposed toward the project, believed he could not go against the advice of his official staff.

Senator Hale started to percolate some action in Washington — but let Dorr tell it:

> Senator Hale at once took a hand and got the Navy Department to send down again Captain Hooper, chief of the opposing experts, with instructions not to return without coming to some settlement of the problem.
>
> Congressman Nelson, going to the Navy Department's rooms, sought Captain Hooper out and had a frank talk with him. It must have been a truly frank talk, for Captain Hooper said:
>
> "You insult me!"
>
> "I mean to," said Congressman Nelson.
>
> But they parted friends. . . .
>
> Captain Hooper, when he reached Bar Harbor, was still determined to retain the Otter Cliffs site, though ready, with the promise of a new building, to shift, within certain bounds, the position of the station.

The day of his arrival was cold and rainy, with mists rolling in from the sea, but he kept the whole party out with him in the dripping woods at Otter Creek, exploring the terrain for an alternate site. In the afternoon, clothes dried and the inner man restored, we met again at the office of Mr. Harry Lynam, acting alike for the Government and for Mr. Rockefeller, and Captain Hooper made various proposals for changing the building — not the site. And he insisted that if Mr. Rockefeller only understood what he proposed, he would yield at once. Mr. Lynam arranged for him to talk direct with Mr. Rockefeller and the wire to New York was held open for half an hour; but it was all to no avail. Mr. Rockefeller would not yield an inch.

The next morning we met once more in Mr. Lynam's office. The day again was rainy and disagreeable. Captain Hooper announced that he had explored every possibility. No solution could be found, he said, and he was ready to return to Washington.

"Captain Hooper," I said, "you were sent down here from Secretary Adams' office with instruction not to return without coming to some agreement. You have done your best to return without coming to some agreement. You have done your best to retain a site at Otter Cliffs, without success. You have not been over to Schoodic."

"I went over that before," he said, "and reported adversely on it. It will not do."

"I know about your visit to Schoodic," I replied, "and the spirit in which you made it. You came determined in advance to turn the proposition down. Your report was biased and you made no fair investigation. You cannot return to Washington now, under the instructions you have received, without at least visiting the Schoodic site again."

And reluctantly he consented.

Mr. Walters G. Hill, our engineer who had helped on the road survey and the search for water, offered to take Captain Hooper over with his junior assistant from the Boston Navy Yard in his car, which was waiting at the door. They went, accordingly, and before they reached the half-way mark, the skies cleared, the sun came out, shining bright and warm. Mr. Hill drove rapidly and before the Navy man realized it they had reached Schoodic. Mr. Hill and the junior engineer walked on ahead while Captain Hooper, lame from his exploring trip the day before, declared he would remain behind, but, seeing them disappear, he hobbled after and finally reached the site, finding it pleasant beyond expectation in the October sunshine. He returned and reported on it in an altered mood.

Dorr's difficulties in Maine had vanished; those in Washington began. The National Park Service, lacking his patience and optimism, had come to look upon the Schoodic project as dead and consequently had reserved no funds. The Navy struck a hard bargain. In exchange for consent to move its radio station to the as yet undeveloped Schoodic, it demanded of the Park an access road over difficult, however scenic, peninsula country. It estimated that its needed building alone would cost the Park the tidy sum of $350,000. Door, sharpening his pencil, pared the request down, assuring National Park Director Albright that $250,000 would be sufficient. Together, he and Albright sought out the Director of the Budget to enter the amount required. The estimates for the fiscal year had just gone across to President Hoover, but there was still time. The Director of the Budget, obviously interested, offered to take the National Park request to the President that very afternoon and explain it to him.

This was done, the item entered and the appropriation passed; another day and Dorr would have been "too late." Once more, via the psychological advantage of the last-minute approach, he had whipped up his horse in the closing moments of a stretch drive and hung on for the victory.

But all the necessary marginalia of the Schoodic dream had not been completed — nor, despite all urging on the part of Dorr, were they to be before the coming in of a new administration, beginning with the momentous inauguration of Franklin D. Roosevelt. The new Director of the Budget, Lewis Douglas, impounded all appropriations not secured by contract. After a long series of arguments, Dorr finally persuaded Douglas of the solidity of his request.

Two years later, in 1935, the transfer of the Naval Station from Otter Cliffs to Schoodic Point, across the Bay, had been accomplished; the costly yet beautiful Park road running up to the new building had been completed.

For years Mr. Rockefeller had stood in the wings waiting to begin his extended Ocean Drive, which would continue around Otter Cliffs point and eventually beyond. The conditions he laid down at the beginning had at last been achieved by Dorr. The old Naval station at Otter Point was pulled down, and all that remained of Alessandro Fabbri's great contribution to World War I was marked by a bronze plaque. Mr. Rockefeller would at once commence the stupendous construction, to pass outside the little village of Otter Creek and up through the spruce forests above the granite shore line.

Dorr, now eighty, his failing sight having reached almost the point of no return, betook himself to Washington for a last request concerning the enlargement of his beloved Acadia: he hoped to extend its lands to the western, the "backside" of Mt. Desert Island.

The depression was plunging on. From minds that had concocted such panaceas as the W.P.A. came the establishment of the national Civilian Conservation Camps, planned to create work for a vast group of the younger unemployed on unprofitable lands purchased from the owners by the government. Dorr applied for two such camps, one on the western and the other on the eastern side of the island; the applications were granted, furnishing Acadia National Park with valuable lowcost labor. Thereafter, Dorr was able to acquire more tracts on the western side, where the mountains and forests beyond Somes Sound were of a scenic quality to merit protection.*

In 1935, Dorr was driven to Boston for an operation on his eyes. Arriving early in the Hub, he and his chauffeur hunted all over town for the moment's need, a two-volume edition of Spinoza. This found, Dorr entered the hospital.

*Dorr had already suffered his first heart attack. The C. C. C. boys, when alerted that the octogenarian would be inspecting their domains, stationed themselves behind trees and boulders in case he fell.

The surgery was performed successfully; Dorr returned to Bar Harbor bearing distinct instructions from his ophthalmologist not to follow his usual custom of reading outdoors in bright sunlight. This advice he studiously avoided, in fact reading all the more in the brightness at an accelerated rate. And why? His only answer: "I must make up for time recently lost." The irrational practice was typical of a vital stubborness; in low shoes, for example, he would slosh through a puddle rather than step around it. The reading fetish took its toll: within a year he had lost all vision, except to discern a shadowy difference between light and darkness.

Thomas Vint of the National Park Service in Washington recalls visiting Dorr at Oldfarm and enjoying himself hugely, despite his host's inability to see. One night after dinner, Dorr, in full voice, was regaling his guest with tales of a pirate ancestor, in whose deeds the host took great pride. Dorr crossed the room to a library shelf and meticulously, with one finger, counted off a certain number of books to the right and plucked forth the exact binding he sought, a volume on the old pirate, which he presented to his house guest.

Dorr was a sturdy swimmer, churning regularly in Bar Harbor's subnormally cold sea water, which even in the hottest days felt as frigid as if full of floating ice blocks. Such temperatures could not deter his daily plunge. Cleveland Amory tells an apocryphal story in *The Last Resorts:*

> Dorr was a life-long bachelor who devoted not only his entire career, but also his personal fortune to the establishment of the Park. He reached his strategic heights at a vital meeting in Washington when a skeptical congressman asked him if Bar Harbor wasn't too cold for swimming. Dorr, at the time nearing seventy, glared at the man. "Sir," he said, "I swim every day until Christmas." Dorr failed to add, of course, that he was the only Mount Deserter, resorter or native, who ever performed such a feat — and the appropriation was granted.

According to members of his staff, he would break the ice to maintain the ritual of his daily dip.

One morning in 1934, when he was occupying the Storm Beach Cottage, Dorr was gone, it seemed, overlong during his usual swimming period. Mrs. Phyllis Sylvia, his secretary and general factotum, scented trouble and sent his chauffeur down onto the rocks. There was the old man, lying unconscious across a ledge, with the incoming tide only a few inches away. Carried back to the house and a doctor summoned, he was diagnosed as the victim of a severe heart attack, with but six months to live — a pronouncement Dorr was to prove wrong by nine and a half years. On recovering from the setback, he frequently ran upstairs to prove he could; he insisted that the heart muscle could be strengthened only by hard exercise.

Dorr was a stickler for punctuality unless his own presence was required at a specific time. His punctual, youthful chauffeur, Dana Young, had left the Park service in 1927 to drive Dorr's old Essex car. The daily routine, according to Young, was to pick up Mrs. Sylvia and the cook each morning, arriving

View from Manset looking back at Southwest Harbor and Northeast. Well at left is the mouth of Somes Sound and is believed to be the meadow site of luckless Jesuit Mission of 1613. Manset gets its name from a distortion of Mansell. Sir Thomas Mansell, Vice Admiral in his Majesty's Navy, bought the island from the crown for 100 pounds. Like Sir Francis Bernard, he did nothing specific regarding his claim.

at the Dorr house at eight sharp. If the trio occasionally happened to be a few minutes late, they would find the tall figure out on the lawn, his remonstrating watch in one hand, while the other attempted vainly to draw his blowing robe together over pajama tops which never seemed to be affixed to the bottoms.

Inside the house, the cook would prepare breakfast. Mrs. Sylvia would type on a card a list of the master's appointments for the day; this was handed over to the security of Young, who would do his best to see that Dorr adhered to the schedule. Some days Dorr would spend at paperwork. Generally, however, he had Young drive him to the edge of some favorite hike, with instructions to meet at a distant point miles and hours away. Such tramps usually lasted well through the lunch hour. Dorr always fortified the inner man by carrying one or two crackers in his pocket.

A. Stroud Rodick, told how Dorr lured him more than once out of his busy office or away from his warming hearth. "Next thing I knew, we'd be on top of some mountain on his promise that the trip would take but a few minutes. At such times I was horribly late for meals. As for Dorr, it was a wonder any hostess ever asked him anywhere." But hardly any social dinner was held in Bar Harbor without Dorr in attendance, at which times his huge appetite would make up for short rations earlier.

Living next to David Ogden, noted New York lawyer and a man of tremendous intellect, Dorr was a permanent guest in the Ogden house. He had a standing invitation for Sunday-night supper; a tray was always ready for him, bearing all the courses for which Dorr had failed to appear on time. Some years after Ogden died, the Sunday bidding was rescinded. It seems that Dorr needed to acquire for Mr. Rockefeller some land left to Mrs. Ogden in the Otter Cliffs region so that a coastal road might continue its unbroken way; she cared not to sell. This so irked Dorr that he impulsively possessed the land via his right of eminent domain. But in later years the incident was forgotten. Mrs. Ogden, like so many others, became tolerant of the earnest gentleman in his blindness, making frequent calls in order to read to him — a practice he considered a blessed favor.

Likewise, in his last years there came to Oldfarm such friends as Mrs. Edward Browning, Mrs. Ernesto G. Fabbri, Mrs. Lea McI. Luquer, Miss Frances Coleman, Ambassador Henry Morgenthau and a score of others and such distinguished former foes as Lincoln Cromwell, who was to donate Dog and Robinson Mountains (now St. Sauveur and Acadia, respectively), on the western side of Somes Sound, to Dorr's Park. Harold Peabody, embittered years ago by the incessant building of Mr. Rockefeller's horse roads, let bygones be, in favor of his overruling respect for the old warrior.

In the Park publications Dorr wrote authoritatively on forestry and geology. In the realm of bird lore, however, he depended on the knowledge of Henry Lane Eno. Eno in the early twenties had himself contributed substantially and encouraged others to donate to the welfare of the Park superintendent; by this time the decline of the latter's family textile holdings, plus his own unrestricted spending in behalf of Mt. Desert Island, had brought a once sizable fortune to the vanishing point.

Mme. Paul Marthelot, whom Dorr had known since her early girlhood, had married a charming French cavalry officer; she especially delighted Dorr when she read in beautiful French from favorite novels. One day she appeared at Oldfarm out of a rain shower. Dorr touched her dripping hat with his hand.

"I can't see you, dear Catherine," he said, "but I can understand why everyone says that you are more handsome than ever."

Many years before, Dorr had not been so gallant in the presence of Catherine Porter. Once the young people of the island got over being afraid of him — his was a forbidding appearance accentuated by walrus mustaches, his huge figure encased in bulgy tweeds — they enjoyed his wit and gruff kindness and shared his childlike worship of the outdoors, the lichen and the birds. He often took the two Porter sisters on extended walks. One day he was climbing Dog Mountain, accompanied by Catherine; the little miss, trying to keep up with Dorr's onrushing pace, fell on reaching the summit and badly twisted her ankle. She remembers that Dorr, entranced with the view, paid her no attention, and that somehow, in great pain, she managed to make the descent.

She was abed the next morning, recovering from her injury, when Dorr was announced. He burst into the room and presented the young lady with a mammoth bunch of roses, two dozen selected from his Mt. Desert Nurseries. "My dear," he exclaimed, "yesterday your courage was superb!"

The Mt. Desert Nurseries, which Dorr owned, suffered a sad financial end due to the questionable direction of its manager. Returning home after an extended trip abroad, Dorr was staggered with the news that the operator to whom he had given power of attorney had piled mortgage upon mortgage and milked the nursery dry.

The National Archives in Washington retain at least thirteen jumbo-size files of official Dorr correspondence. One brief note of the year 1932, following a visit by the director of the National Park Service, reveals a willingness to accept an expense-account remuneration for $2.

Department of the Interior
National Park Service
Acadia National Park
Bar Harbor, Maine

July 16, 1932

OFFICE OF THE SUPERINTENDENT
The Director,
National Park Service,
Washington, D.C.

Dear Mr. Director:
As requested in Service letter of July 14, 1932, I am enclosing bill from the MacLeod's Garage, Bar Harbor, amounting to $2.25, for the storage of Secretary Wilbur's car, in connection with his recent visit to Acadia National Park.

Very truly yours,
George B. Dorr,
Superintendent.

Near the end, it was pathetic to see Dorr's impoverished state. He would cut off the end of frayed cuffs or perhaps patch up a once superb Bond Street suit to attend some official Park meeting. But he himself felt his unaccustomed poverty only in not being able to order from the book lists that came to his attention each month. The single time Mrs. Sylvia ever saw him burst forth in acerbity was when, as watchdog of his now meager capital, she had to dissuade him from buying a choice selection of new tomes. She never heard him complain of his blindness, Dana Young but once. In the lobby of Portland's Hotel Eastland, the blind Dorr tripped at the head of a trio of terraced staircases and was about to plunge full length when saved by a flying tackle from the ever watchful chauffeur-

Dividing Southwest Harbor from Tremont is this serpentine brook. Western Mountains in distance.

Birch Harbor on the Schoodic side near Acadia. Patch of lobstermen, rear.

attendant. Pulling himself together, Dorr muttered, "This accursed darkness!"

Otherwise he asserted that he would much rather be blind than unable to hear. If the members of his household had troubles, they would bring them to

Dorr. The old man reveled in illuminating the downcast spirits of others, transmitting mirth and encouragement from his own never-ending supply.

In the blind years, Oldfarm was fitted out with a system of hand rails running from room to room. It was across one of these that the courageous soul fell just before dawn on August 5, 1944, in an attempt to reach his bath. The heart that had been supposed to stop nine years before finally gave in.

To his memory was erected a simple tablet alongside Sieur de Monts Spring. The dedication ceremonies included words to the effect that the bronze and stone plaque would outlast the ravages of time. But the renowned Bar Harbor Fire, sweeping in its greatest intensity through the spring glade, melted the monument as if it had been made of plastic.

Today a new relief stands near the former one. It reads:

IN MEMORY OF
GEORGE BUCKNAM DORR
1853 - 1944
GENTLEMAN SCHOLAR
LOVER OF NATURE
FATHER OF THIS
NATIONAL PARK
STEADFAST IN HIS ZEAL TO MAKE THE BEAUTIES
OF THIS ISLAND
AVAILABLE TO ALL

Strangely, the fire left untouched the little Italian Renaissance well-house over the famous spring, which Dorr had so pridefully installed forty years before. The other Porter sister, Margaretta, tells of once being taken to Sieur de Monts by Dorr. He asked her opinion of the new, formal covering. She hesitated; she had fond memories of visiting the spring with her father and watching him plunge a long, pointed branch into the pool to make it bubble up with all its amazing effervescence. To create such a phenomenon would be impossible now that the water was to be seen through glass. "Oh, Mr. Dorr," she said, "why didn't you leave it as God made it?" For some time she would be the recipient of stony silences and stern looks.

Many of the younger summer rich were even more tactless concerning the changes. Undoubtedly their early opinions of the bushy man had been shaped by overhearing their parents denigrate his practice of exposing their special haunts to aliens, the "trippers." At night, now and again, aristocratic youthful voices would call under a sleeping Dorr's window, "Oh, Mr. Dorr! Don't change the names of the mountains. Don't change them. Don't!" The same imps would then pull up the stakes set out to mark the beginnings of a new road.

Just as no one can please all the people all of the time, no one stayed angry at Dorr for very long. He had seen the world and realized that Mt. Desert was a realm apart; he also knew greedy mankind, and that insensitive landowners could sometime make a honkytonk of these beautiful acres. He would see to it that man was protected against his own destructive hand.

Sieur De Monts Spring. The Italian Renaissance well cover was installed by George B. Dorr near the beginning of this century.

Bishop Lawrence at the Congratulatory Meeting at The Building of Arts in 1916 had said: "Now no one can come down and spoil the lands the Government has taken under its protection. No fire can sweep though them." Thirty years later the Bar Harbor Fire almost did. Dorr died three years before the Great Fire. Had he been alive at the time, his blind eyes could not have seen the destruction in the park, but he would have sensed the blackened stench more keenly than others.

Dorr applied his hearty sense of humor to his blindness. Once his loyal chauffeur found him reflecting, with a sad smile, on the ruthless trimming given him by the shears of a local barber, new to the assignment. The huge man was wryly attempting to twist the short ends of what had formerly been a wild growth of great, drooping mustaches.

"He skinned me!" grinned Dorr, totally blind. "I can hardly recognize myself."

Driven about the Park in an automobile, he was always aware of his geographical position. Suddenly he would order the car stopped and point out to the occupants the features of a favorite view. Some kind of built-in radar told him that he was on the exact spot he had paused to describe.

In the final days, when the old man's holdings had shrunk almost to the vanishing point (and would have disappeared had Dorr known his true worth, however infinitesimal) Serenus Rodick, trustee, told Dorr's attendant that he (Rodick) had "stolen" $2,000 from Dorr to set aside for funeral expenses and various inevitable last expenditures, and that he wanted someone to bear witness to his act.

The giant whose talents death was not to hide was cremated with all the honors of simplicity due a great man, and with all the loose ends of obligation wrapped up neatly and tidily.* In keeping with his request, Ben Hadley and Serenus Rodick, designated friends, scattered his ashes on the hillside behind the Storm Beach Cottage. The lovely antique furniture and the Lowestoft services inherited from his mother went by private sale into the houses of Bar Harbor residents.

Today, thirty-four years after Dorr's death, the park that started with 5,000

138

acres has grown to about 35,000 acres, including Schoodic Peninsula, the larger portion of Isle au Haut, and a number of small offshore islands. In 1970 Mrs. David Rockefeller started the Maine Coast Heritage Trust. The trust seeks conservation easements to protect land surrounding the Park from heavy and undesirable development. At this writing, Acadia holds more than 80 easements. Over 3,000,000 visits are made to the park yearly compared with 680,000 in the first post-World War II year, 1946.

A well-planned interpretive Naturalist Program, scheduled from July 1 through August 31, offers bird walks, geology hikes, ecology walks, mountain hikes, an introduction to orienteering, an astronomy watch, sea cruises and campfire programs. This program is carried out by nine Park Naturalists during the summer months, assisted by a staff of student conservation assistants.

Almost fifty species of mammals inhabit the park during the course of the year.* It is, of course, illegal to collect or damage wildlife within the park, and deer cannot be legally killed anywhere on Mt. Desert.

It has been stated by ornithologist James Bond that our knowledge of the native birds surpasses that of any area of comparable size and diversity of avifauna in Maine or any other New England state. Indeed, the island is one of Roger Tory Peterson's "dozen birding hot spots," as described in a recently published book of that title. Of the 138 species listed as indigenous to the area, Mt. Desert is justly renowned for its variety of wood warblers; twenty-one warblers are regarded as summer residents. A useful checklist, compiled by Paul Favour, may be obtained at Park Headquarters at Hull's Cove. This list, which includes 314 species and four subspecies, contains an interesting mixture of Canadian and Southern birds; the latter have increased partly due to the change in environment resulting from the fire. Southwestern Mt. Desert has more northern birds, the northeastern part of the island more southern birds.

Visitors to the park ask more questions about wildflowers than any other phase of natural history. More than 500 kinds of flowering plants and many types of mosses, lichens, and lesser plants adorn the island's varied habitats — deciduous and evergreen forests, roadsides and trailsides, exposed rocky shore and mountaintops (where conditions approximate those further north), meadows, ponds and their later stages, peat bogs and heaths.

At Sieur de Monts Spring, a flat and formerly unprepossing three-fourths of an acre has been developed as the "Wild Gardens of Acadia." Mr. Dorr named it

---

*Well, perhaps not so tidily. Miss Claudia Phelps who lived in one of the fine old houses on the Bar Harbor shore close by the Storm Beach Cottage told this story as gospel truth: a score of years ago she and her mother were enjoying an August al fresco lunch on the piazza overlooking the sea when a small plane began slowly circling overhead. Soon mysterious debris began to fall into their demitasse cups.

Suddenly Mrs. Phelps turned ashen.

"Oh dear," she exclaimed, hectically wiping her face with her napkin — "It's Mr. Dorr!"

"It seemed so cannibalistic," said Miss Phelps, recounting the incident.

Mr. Dorr, late as usual for lunch, had, true to form, made his presence eventful.

*For a description of these and other fauna, the reader is referred to Dale Rex Coman's *The Native Mammals, Reptiles and Amphibians of Mount Desert Island, Maine,* Bar Harbor, 1972.

such in 1916 and incorporated it "for educational and scientific purposes," but it did not become reality until 1960 when the idea was revived by Harold A. Hubler, then Park Superintendent, who invited the Bar Harbor Garden Club to undertake the project. The work of planning, organizing, studying, collecting (from other sources since collection is not permitted within the park), propagating, planting, labeling, and fund raising has been accomplished by volunteers. Today over 200 indigenous species of plants, shrubs, and trees may be viewed in ten habitats designed and constructed to duplicate the plants' natural environment. Truly, a botanical treasure trove!

A staff of approximately 20 seasonal Park Rangers carries out a program of protection for both the visitors to the Park* and the natural features of the area. To adequately maintain the roads, (including the 55 miles of carriage roads, created by John D. Rockefeller, Jr.), the 120 miles of trails, the picnic sites, campgrounds, and other facilities, it is necessary to employ forty maintenance men during the heavy use season.

Since the death of Mr. Dorr, two campgrounds — Black Woods and Seawall — with a total of 572 sites plus ten group sites have been developed. The use of these campgrounds has grown steadily; from 886 camper days in 1944 to 239,685 camper days in 1977.

In recent years, increasing numbers of winter enthusiasts are enjoying the snow-laden woods and mountains of Mt. Desert. About thirty miles of carriage paths in Acadia National Park have been reserved for the quiet joys of snowshoeing and cross country skiing. The not-so-quiet snowmobilers are allowed to operate on that section of the Loop Road between Scenic Overlook Road and Otter Cliffs Road.

The millions of visitors, past, present, and future, who have or will come to Acadia to escape the anxieties of modern living and there to find renewal by intimacy with nature, owe a debt of gratitude to George Bucknam Dorr. In the last paragraph of his charming *The Story of Mount Desert Island*, the late Samuel Eliot Morison, historian, sailor, and island summer resident, wrote what could well have been the everlasting sentiment of the Park's first caretaker:

> But we who love this Island say that it can never be ruined while the tide ebbs and flows twice a day and an offshore wind turns the sea into an incredible blue, or the east wind brings wreaths of fog that clothe the coasts and hills in soft white. It can never be ruined while Acadia National Park keeps up its trails. . . . Mount Desert is not merely an Island; it is a way of life to which one becomes addicted; and if we are permitted in the hereafter to enter that abode where the just are made perfect, let us hope that it may have some resemblance to Champlain's Isle des Monts Deserts.

---

*Yearly the Park Rangers rescue some terror stricken adventurer on a mountain cliff unable to go either forward or backward. Shore line Park warnings are too often ignored. Almost every summer there has been a tourist swept away by an engulfing wave when too closely viewing surf phenomena off Thunder Hole or elsewhere along the Ocean Drive.

Of Mice and Men and Human Ecology
The Jackson Laboratory

T HE Jackson Laboratory was born in 1929 and named in memory of Roscoe B. Jackson, former president of the Hudson Motor Car Company and long-time summer resident of Seal Harbor. Its stated purpose is "to increase man's knowledge of himself, of his development, growth, and reproduction, of his physiological and psychological behavior, and of his inborn ailments, through research with genetically controlled experimental animals."

Its founder and first director was Clarence Cook Little, a direct descendent of Paul Revere, who once headed the Universities of Maine and Michigan. In 1929 Dr. Little was armed with eight employees, scanty laboratory equipment, and a budget of $50,000. Today, the laboratory employs over 450 local individuals twelve months of the year (which gives it Hancock County's second largest payroll), and is the base of some thirty-five scientists with doctoral degrees. Its 1978 budget was $10,000,000.

Weathering the great Depression (with the aid of kitchen garden produce for its workers and their families and strict economizing), the laboratory's reputation grew quickly. In 1938 it received the first two research grants awarded by the new National Cancer Institute.

The Great Fire of 1947 gutted the Jackson buildings, destroyed 90,000 inbred mice, hundreds of valuable records, and all of the research equipment. A few days following the fire, "Pete" Little was seen pursuing his relentless way through the asphalt canyons of New York City, hatless, his handsome face bearing the messianic look. Briefcase in hand, the familiar pipe compressed between his lips, he was seeking new capital for a soon-to-be-rebuilt Jackson Laboratory. The structure that arose from the rubble soon grew to be several times its original size, its mouse population restored with pairs donated by research workers from all over the world.

Today, the laboratory produces annually some 3,000,000 mice of which about two-thirds are shipped to other scientists and laboratories in more than twenty countries. From the lab's mouse colony, research workers can order mice with high cancer rate or low cancer rate; mice afflicted with muscular dystrophies or anemias; or mice with a wide range of other specific inherited characteristics. Sixty-seven inbred strains and over 400 mutants have been developed.

Many-faceted cancer research amounts to about 40 per cent of the institution's research effort; the mice (and other laboratory animals) are also being asked to answer questions relating to a broad range of other inborn or constitutional diseases — diabetes, muscular dystrophies, transplantation immunity, metabolic disorders, aging and behavior, as well as basic biological problems.

Besides research and mouse-rearing, each summer the laboratory conducts a nine-week training program for high school seniors and a concurrent ten-week program for college students. Competition for the programs is intense: last summer, 179 students applied for the high school program (15 were accepted) and 164 sought entry in the college session (22 made it). There were also eleven pre- and postdoctoral fellows at the laboratory last summer. Under the training program each student tackles a research project under the supervision of a sponsoring scientist.*

From mid-June to mid-September, three days a week, the laboratory offers a visitors' program, which includes a film and a speaker. In 1976 Dr. Richmond T. Prehn assumed directorship of the institution, succeeding Dr. Earl Green, the laboratory's second director.

Scientists and technicians consider Mt. Desert a particularly fortunate location for the laboratory, explaining its tranquillity (at least ten months of the year) is conducive to studious concentration. Dr. Little once put it thus:

> "In such work, Maine, both by its simple, natural beauty, its ruggedness and the quality of its people, who help as general assistants and in actual research, is an ideal setting. Most creative effort of man's mind and spirit seeks quiet and isolation for its birth and growth. Maine possesses these opportunities which mark it as perhaps the most privileged of all the. . . states under our flag."

---

*The Nobel Prize in medicine in 1975 went to two young scientists, Drs. Howard Temin and David Baltimore, who independently determined that the rules for the transmission of genetic information within the cell could be reversed. Twenty years earlier they both took part in the laboratory's training program for precollege students.

C.C. ("Prexy" or "Pete") Little with
feathered friend.

The Mount Desert Island Biological
Laboratory

First in age of the Bar Harbor laboratories is the Mount Desert Island
Biological Laboratory in Salisbury Cove, founded in 1893 and removed to its
present location in 1921 when the site was donated by the Wild Gardens of
Acadia. Its fundamental studies of biological phenomena are based mainly on fish
or other salt and fresh water species. Originally operating only during the
summer months, since 1972 it has been a year-round facility.

During 1976 there were 117 scientific personnel in 38 research groups,
representing 56 institutions both here and abroad, including 57 professional
scientists and 60 students, technicians, and staff. They work and are housed in
some 35 small, simple frame buildings, the earliest of which were constructed or
obtained by the gifts of local summer residents. These buildings are spread out
along the shore and in the woods of a beautiful cove area of about 150 acres
bordering upper Frenchman Bay.

The rocky shores, mud flats, and strong tidal currents provide a large variety
of marine forms, including the otherwise scorned sculpin and goosefish. Because
of their anatomical structure, these have proven to be most valuable in providing
data that aid our understanding of kidney function, not only in fish but in higher
animals and man. Many world-renowned renal physiologists, notably the late

Homer W. Smith, E. K. Marshall, and others, worked here for more than 30 years and during that period have revolutionized our understanding of how the kidney works. Mt. Desert Island should be proud to have played a vital role in this triumph of modern physiology.

Salt and fresh water fish, invertebrates and their eggs, many of them taken from the ocean and fresh water ponds, serve as the basic tools of the laboratory's research. The dogfish, a small shark, is available in good supply. Unsaleable and consequently detested by local fishermen, it is a favorite of the investigators at Salisbury Cove.

The weekly seminars at the laboratory include erudite topics, most of which are too professional and specialized for the lay summer visitor, e.g., "The Role of the Kidney in the Evolution of Terrestrial Animals from Water-Dwelling Ancestors," "Intrarenal Pressure," and "Glomerular Intermittency." Those who crave the succulent red crustacean might feel a closer rapport with the treatise "The General Form of Circulation in the Lobster."

In the main, investigators' efforts have been directed to fundamental problems of biology and medicine, especially renal and developmental physiology and disease. Timely investigations are also being conducted on the mechanisms of toxicity of chemical pollutants. However, the actual treatment or cure of disease is only the valuable by-product of such research, not the main objective; most investigators of fundamental scientific problems press onward in the search for new knowledge because of curiosity as to how things work.

The determined men and women of the Biological Laboratory bring to this island an amazing breadth and depth of scientific talent. Leaders in many fields, they give up their summer days, and often nights, to further the advance of science. Living and working together for one or many successive summers creates an atmosphere that stimulates ideas and promotes discovery. The pleasant summer climate and friendly local populace of Salisbury Cove make an intangible but real contribution toward these happy results.

College of the Atlantic

Twenty acres of shoreline just outside Bar Harbor and within walking distance of Acadia National Park provide the setting for one of America's most unusual colleges — College of the Atlantic.

The college was conceived of in the late 1960's by a group of island residents, including Bar Harbor businessman Leslie Brewer and the Reverend James Gower, both of whom played prominent roles. At a time when most colleges were being forced to retrench, the college opened its doors in 1972 with thirty-two students. Today, College of the Atlantic is an accredited four-year college awarding a degree of Bachelor of Arts in Human Ecology. "Human ecology" is a broad study. COA's first catalog explained:

Students construct a combination solar lab and greenhouse at the College of the Atlantic.

Rather than beginning with a fixed definition of human ecology, our primary concern will be to develop one. . . . We expect that our concerns will not end with current problems. People will always have difficulty living together as well as in shaping and protecting their natural environment. . . . We will always be concerned with new definitions and problems of human ecology.

Small is still beautiful. Enrollment has steadily grown to 110 students in 1978. The campus now includes, in addition to its main building (formerly an Oblate seminary), two greenhouses, a pottery and gas-fired kiln, a solar and wood-heated workshop designed and built by students, 28,000 sq. ft. of vegetable garden space (as might be expected, many of the student body are vegetarians), a small orchard, root cellar, and composting facilities. In addition, the college owns eighty acres of undeveloped land on Strawberry Hill overlooking Bar Harbor, and a neighboring estate on Frenchman Bay, the Turrets, will be in use in 1978.

There are no titles, rank, or tenure at COA. Teachers teach, across disciplinary lines, courses in four resource areas: Environmental Sciences, Social and Cultural Studies, Environmental Design, and Values and Consciousness. Each of these areas is closely integrated with the other three. Three faculty members have put theory into practice by constructing their own solar-heated homes, assisted at each stage by students.

From the beginning, the college has been closely involved with the life of the island community. Most of the students live off-campus in Bar Harbor or elsewhere on the island. The Park turns to COA for assistance with research tasks, and students have worked at the Jackson Laboratory on summer internships.

In 1975 the college played a major role in forming the Coastal Resource

Center to promote the wise use of coastal resources and help demonstrate that economic development *can* be environmentally compatible. The Cranberry School in Bar Harbor, which provides young children and their parents with a lively educational environment, was founded by a group of COA. In addition the college offers guest speakers, a student-run film series, and concerts.

Positions held today by the small gourp of COA graduates include assistant director of the Maine Audubon Society, researcher for shore birds, wildlife technician, conservation education specialist. (The college president, Edward Kaelber, past associate dean and lecturer at the Harvard Graduate School of Education, would like to see *some* of them go into business or banking or railroads.)

Today, College of the Atlantic — innovative, enthusiastic, informal — is an integral part of the community of Mt. Desert Island, within which it continues to grow.